# International Drug Control Law

# International Drug Control Law

## Trends and Reform Challenges

Khalid Tinasti

ANTHEM PRESS

Anthem Press
An imprint of Wimbledon Publishing Company
*www.anthempress.com*

This edition first published in UK and USA 2026
by ANTHEM PRESS
75–76 Blackfriars Road, London SE1 8HA, UK
or PO Box 9779, London SW19 7ZG, UK
and
244 Madison Ave #116, New York, NY 10016, USA



*British Library Cataloguing-in-Publication Data*
A catalogue record for this book is available from the British Library.

*Library of Congress Cataloging-in-Publication Data: 2025944550*
A catalog record for this book has been requested.

ISBN-13: 978-1-83999-570-5 (Pbk)
ISBN-10: 1-83999-570-X (Pbk)

Cover Credit: NLM collections/public domain

This title is also available as an eBook.

# CONTENTS

# FOREWORD

## By César Gaviria, Former President of Colombia, Former Secretary-General of the Organization of American States

The international drug control regime, based on the three core international drug conventions, remains one of the most universally ratified and enduring legal frameworks of the modern era. It reflects a broad and long-standing consensus. No single country can, in isolation, confront the challenges posed by illicit drug markets. Even before the founding of the United Nations, it was recognized that drug-related criminality, propelled by persistent global demand, vast illicit revenues, and powerful criminal organizations, represents a threat not confined within national borders. The international community responded by developing a system that aimed, on the one hand, to suppress the illicit production, trafficking, and non-medical use of drugs, and on the other, to ensure the availability of controlled substances for legitimate medical and scientific purposes.

The creation of this system was a testament to multilateralism and the shared aspirations of the international community. Yet, while its objectives were noble, the implementation of the drug control regime has produced profound negative consequences, consequences that have profoundly impacted individuals, communities, and entire nations.

My own country, Colombia, has experienced this reality in a particularly acute manner. Coca cultivation, a practice with ancient roots among indigenous peoples, became intertwined over time with the global trade in cocaine and the rise of formidable criminal networks. Colombia has invested vast human, financial, and institutional resources in confronting the threat posed by transnational drug trafficking organizations. We have suffered high levels of violence, endured the corrosion of state institutions, and faced sustained external pressure to eradicate illicit cultivation. Nevertheless, Colombia has also demonstrated resilience and leadership, notably through our commitment to strengthening democracy, building peace, and upholding the rule of law. We have remained steadfast in fulfilling our international obligations under the drug control conventions, even as we have sought to adapt our national policies to our evolving realities.

Understanding the complexities of drug control demands more than a technical appreciation of treaties and their legal architecture. It requires a broader historical and political understanding of the origins of the system, the expectations that accompanied its creation, the successes it has achieved, and the shortcomings that have become evident over time. Only through such an informed perspective can we make sense of why the regime has not always achieved its intended objectives, and why it has, in some cases, contributed to new and unforeseen challenges.

This book offers precisely such a perspective. Khalid Tinasti presents a clear, comprehensive, and accessible account of the evolution of international drug control law, from its early roots in the colonial period to the contemporary landscape shaped by United Nations treaties and successive waves of political commitments. He carefully traces the emergence of the global regime, its principal aims, and the mechanisms by which it has been implemented and sustained. Importantly, he does not shy away from confronting the limitations and contradictions that have emerged over time, including the increasing diversification of drug markets, the rise of synthetic substances not easily captured by existing control frameworks, and the security, health, and human rights costs associated with punitive enforcement strategies.

One of the book's most important contributions is its insider perspective on the diplomacy of drug policy. Tinasti draws on his experience within international forums to illuminate the tensions between states, the strategic compromises that have shaped key outcomes, and the persistent resistance to meaningful reform despite mounting evidence of the need for change. His legal analysis brings clarity to the often opaque and complex world of drug control diplomacy, helping readers understand how institutional inertia, divergent national interests, and differing ideological approaches have sustained the current system even as calls for reform have grown louder.

As a public servant who has spent a significant part of my life engaged in efforts to combat drug trafficking and strengthen the institutions of democracy and justice, I am acutely aware of the profound challenges posed by illicit drug markets. I have witnessed the human cost of inflexible, punitive approaches and the need for policies that are grounded in evidence, respectful of human rights, and oriented toward sustainable solutions. Research, critical analysis, and open dialogue are indispensable tools for advancing these goals.

This book represents a valuable contribution to that endeavor. It offers policymakers, scholars, and concerned citizens alike a nuanced understanding of the international drug control system, its achievements, its limitations, and the urgent questions that confront us today. I hope that it will inspire continued reflection, innovation, and cooperation in the search for more effective and humane responses to one of the most enduring challenges of our time.

# INTRODUCTION

## The Emerging Tensions and Challenges to the International Drug Control Regime

The world is not drug-free. On the contrary, the scale and complexity of global drug use, production, and control mechanisms are greater than ever. As of the latest data, an estimated 292 million people worldwide are reported to use drugs, an increase of 20 percent over the past decade. Cannabis remains the most commonly used substance, accounting for 228 million users. The number of people suffering from drug use disorders has risen to 64 million, signaling deepening public health and policy challenges. On the supply side, drug cultivation and production remain highly dynamic. In 2022, global opium poppy cultivation covered approximately 94,000 hectares, a dramatic 70 percent decline largely attributed to the return of the Taliban government in Afghanistan. Conversely, coca bush cultivation rose by 12 percent to reach 355,000 hectares. Cocaine production hit an all-time high in the same year, with more than 2,700 tons manufactured globally, 20 percent more than the previous year and nearly triple the volumes reported in 2013 and 2014, reflecting an expanding market, particularly in Europe. Meanwhile, the appearance of new psychoactive substances (NPS) continues unabated, with 44 new compounds, including synthetic stimulants and cannabinoids, identified on the illegal market in 2022 alone. The criminalization of drug-related behavior remains widespread, with an estimated 6.9 million individuals coming into formal contact with police for drug offenses, with 2.7 million prosecuted and 1.7 million ultimately convicted.[1]

Yet drug control rests on a solid legal foundation, constructed over the course of the twentieth century through a series of multilateral agreements forged in response to the growing complexity of illicit drug production, distribution, and consumption. These agreements, shaped by both cooperation and geopolitical tension, have gradually coalesced into a unified regime aimed at addressing a transnational challenge. The foundational legal instruments, the 1961 Single Convention on Narcotic Drugs (as amended by the 1972 Protocol), the 1971 Convention on Psychotropic Substances, and the 1988 United Nations Convention against Illicit Traffic in Narcotic Drugs and Psychotropic Substances, together form the cornerstone of the global system, one explicitly designed around international cooperation against what is rightly viewed as a borderless trade. Central to this system is a globally harmonized scheduling mechanism that classifies substances based on their medical usefulness and potential for abuse, compelling state parties to enforce domestic controls aligned with these designations. In principle, this structure allocated distinct responsibilities across the supply chain, from countries cultivating drug crops, through transit states, to those where consumption is concentrated. In practice, these treaties have exerted profound influence over national policies and the architecture of international law enforcement. However, long-standing criticisms have persisted. Chief among them are the rigidity of the scheduling framework, the over-criminalization of drug-related conduct, and a conspicuous gap between the system's stated objectives and its measurable outcomes. Crucially, these issues stem less from the treaties' textual inflexibility than from the orthodoxy of their interpretation and the top-down nature of implementation. Rather than allowing local realities to inform global norms, the reverse has been institutionalized. International standards dictate national and local actions, often without accounting for context. This dynamic has led to a growing divergence between legal doctrine and empirical reality, and, in consequence, to increasingly forceful demands for reform.

This book explores this legal system and its establishment, where the calls for a recalibration stem from, based on the negative consequences of drug control that seem to even out its benefits, and the existing legal options for such review, but also why these are difficult to implement in the current environment although attempts have been ongoing for the last two decades.

The first chapter maps the legal foundation of international drug control. From the 1909 Shanghai Opium Commission through the 1961, 1971, and 1988 treaties, it traces a system historically rooted in colonial economic interests, geopolitical concerns, and shifting global attitudes toward psychoactive substances. These conventions laid the groundwork for today's policies, creating mechanisms for control, enforcement, and intergovernmental cooperation. At their core, they offer a standardized approach to drug policy, mandating criminalization of non-medical drug activities and restricting substances deemed to have little or no therapeutic value even when they are essential to health systems. While influential, they are not immune to critique, especially for entrenching punitive responses and overlooking any other credible alternatives.

Chapter 2 highlights the mounting tensions in implementation. Despite being among the most widely ratified treaties in the world, international drug laws have been unable to halt the growth of global drug markets. Instead, prohibition has contributed to several systemic side effects that even the

United Nations recognizes as "unintended consequences." These include policy distortion, militarized enforcement, the displacement of production and violence, and the stigmatization of drug consumers. Moreover, the control regime now clashes with other pillars of international law, including human rights, health, and development. Its frameworks promote incarceration over treatment, punishment over support, and restrictions over equitable access for legitimate use. The result is a regime increasingly at odds with other international norms and evidence-based practices.

Chapter 3 shifts the focus to the future. What legal avenues exist for reform? Despite increasing acknowledgment that the existing conventions may no longer be fit for purpose, reform remains elusive. The key treaties are entrenched in the architecture of global multilateralism. The 1961 Convention alone has 154 signatories, while the 1988 Convention boasts near-universal ratification with 192 parties. Reform mechanisms are technically available but politically and diplomatically fraught. The international debate, especially regarding cannabis legalization, illustrates this tension. Several states have moved ahead with domestic legalization despite treaty obligations, reflecting a growing disconnect between legal orthodoxy and political reality. Still, viable reform options, ranging from treaty amendment to reinterpretation, face stiff resistance from those invested in the status quo.

Mainly, this book offers a succinct analysis of the international drug control regime, outlining its historical evolution and current complexities. It examines the unintended consequences of drug control policies, which, in many cases, overshadow the intended benefits. However, the book refrains from advocating for reform, recognizing that the political and legal pathways to such change are constrained. Reform seems improbable, as no clear political avenue currently exists to alter the entrenched framework of international drug law.

This book is grounded in a realistic appraisal of the situation. On one hand, there is a broad, international agreement on the need to address drug-related issues, resulting in a unified legal system. On the other, the enforcement of these policies has led to significant negative effects, particularly in the realms of human rights and public health. Despite these drawbacks, the international system persists, operating on a lowest-common-denominator approach that reflects competing national interests rather than a shared, comprehensive solution.

Ultimately, this work aims to provide a clear, focused overview of the current state of global drug control. It does not propose easy solutions, as no single response exists. Rather, it attempts to distill a complex policy area into a coherent understanding of where the world stands today on drug control, facing challenges that have proven difficult to overcome and showing little sign of meaningful reform.

# Chapter 1

# UNDERSTANDING THE INTERNATIONAL DRUG CONTROL NORMATIVE FRAMEWORK

The international drug control regime is built upon a series of key treaties that have shaped global drug policy and that were codified over the past century to respond to the emerging challenges of illegal drugs. The three core conventions (the 1961 Single Convention on Narcotic Drugs [as amended by the 1972 Protocol], the 1971 Convention on Psychotropic Substances, and the 1988 United Nations Convention against Illicit Traffic in Narcotic Drugs and Psychotropic Substances) form the legal framework governing the production, distribution, trafficking, medical and scientific use, trade, and consumption of controlled substances. These treaties established a system of scheduling substances based on their medical value and potential for abuse and diversion, influencing both national policies and international enforcement mechanisms. While designed to streamline drug control measures and curb illegal markets, the conventions have also faced criticism for their rigid classifications, political influences in scheduling decisions, and limited effectiveness of their provisions' implementation in reducing global drug use and trafficking.

The origins of international drug control trace back to the early twentieth century, deeply intertwined with the legacy of the Opium Wars and the subsequent economic and social instability in China, spurring the first international regulatory efforts, culminating in the 1909 Shanghai Opium Commission. This gathering marked the beginning of multilateral drug control discussions, setting the stage for the Hague Opium Convention of 1912 and subsequent treaties (Geneva Conventions of 1925, 1931, and 1936 under the League of Nations) leading up to the modern drug control framework. The historical context of drug control is essential to understanding the evolution of current policies, as it reflects a broader narrative of economic interests, geopolitical power struggles, and shifting perspectives on drug use and regulation.

## The Three Drug Conventions and the Scheduling of Substances, the Cornerstone of the International Drug Control Regime

International drug control has evolved through the adoption of three key treaties that form the basis of the international drug control regime: (1) the 1961 Single Convention on Narcotic Drugs, as amended by the 1972 Protocol; (2) the 1971 Convention on Psychotropic Substances; (3) and the 1988 United Nations Convention against Illicit Traffic in Narcotic Drugs and Psychotropic Substances. These conventions define the international legal framework governing drug control policies.[1]

The Single Convention on Narcotic Drugs of 1961 was designed to unify, supersede, and streamline previous international drug control treaties adopted between 1912 and 1953 (The Hague Opium Convention of 1912 and the Geneva Conventions of 1925, 1931, and 1936, and the Opium Protocol of 1953). It consolidated various agreements into a single legal framework, simplifying regulations and extending the scope of control measures. While it maintained the focus on controlling drug supply, it introduced significant regulatory shifts.

The convention resulted from negotiations among participating states, each bringing national priorities shaped by their roles in the global drug market and broader geopolitical factors. The treaty pursued three main objectives: (1) the simplification of previous control mechanisms, (2) the expansion of control measures to include additional substances and their derivatives, (3) and strengthening drug control by extending regulations to raw materials used for narcotic drug production.[2]

The Single Convention solidified the principle of limiting narcotic drugs to medical and scientific purposes, as stated in its Article 4. It introduced a classification system grouping substances into four Schedules based on their perceived medical value and abuse potential.[3] Notably, many report that classification decisions were influenced by non-scientific considerations, arguing it is evidenced by the inclusion of coca leaf and cannabis in restrictive schedules based on limited field studies.[4]

The convention also marked a change from earlier regulatory approaches by incorporating prohibitionist principles. While prior agreements primarily restricted trade and production, the 1961 framework required states to exercise control over consumers, incorporating treatment and rehabilitation measures. Additionally, the treaty mandated the elimination of traditional uses of controlled plants within a specified timeline (Article 49). Countries party to the Single Convention were mandated to abolish opium use within 15 years and cannabis and coca leaf use within 25 after the entry in force of the treaty in 1964.[5] This means for example that non-medical cannabis use and coca leaf chewing should have disappeared by 1989, and that our generation should not know what using these drugs recreationally means. The International Narcotics Control Board (INCB) was established to oversee compliance, merging two previous oversight bodies, the Permanent Central Opium Board (PCOB) and the Drug Supervisory Body (DSB).[6] The convention largely maintained a supply-control focus, with limited provisions addressing demand reduction, which were later introduced through the 1972 Protocol.

Following the adoption of the treaty on narcotic drugs, the widespread non-medical use of synthetic psychoactive substances, including amphetamines, benzodiazepines, and barbiturates, necessitated an expanded regulatory framework. Unlike earlier treaties focused on plant-based narcotics, the 1971 Convention on Psychotropic Substances introduced controls over synthetic drugs. A notable shift in negotiating positions occurred, with states producing plant-based drugs favoring strict international controls over synthetic substances similar to the ones on opium, coca leaf, and cannabis, while industrialized states with strong pharmaceutical sectors sought a more flexible approach.[7] The resulting agreement maintained a tiered scheduling system, but with a fundamental difference from the 1961 Convention. A substance would be controlled only if scientific evidence demonstrated a significant risk of abuse (Article 2.4). This was a departure from the 1961 treaty where the principle was that a substance is to be classified in the most restrictive schedule in case of doubt on its potential harms. The treaty also acknowledged certain traditional and ritual uses of psychoactive substances.[8] Article 32.4 allowed reservations for plants used in religious or cultural contexts, a provision that several states invoked upon ratification. Nonetheless, many active compounds from such plants, including mescaline, psilocybin, and tetrahydrocannabinol, were placed under international control.

By the 1980s, concerns over the scale of international drug trafficking led to the negotiation of the 1988 United Nations Convention Against Illicit Traffic in Narcotic Drugs and Psychotropic Substances. The treaty reflected a growing consensus that drug trafficking required enhanced international cooperation, although perspectives on causality diverged. Drug-producing and transit states argued that demand from high-consumption countries was the primary driver, while consumer states emphasized the need for eradication efforts in producer regions.[9] The 1988 Convention significantly expanded the scope of international drug control by criminalizing a broad range of drug-related activities. Article 3 required state parties to criminalize activities related to production, distribution, and possession, extending criminal liability to people who use drugs under certain conditions.[10] The convention also established legal frameworks for asset forfeiture, precursor chemical control, and extradition to facilitate law enforcement cooperation.

Despite the comprehensive legal architecture, the impact of international drug conventions on reducing drug production, trafficking, and consumption remains limited. International data gathered in the annual World Drug Report indicate that global illegal drug markets have expanded despite enforcement measures, and that such expansion has been steady since the publication of this global data in the late 1990s to today.[11]

The conventions are also the international regulatory texts for access to essential controlled medicines, prescribed for pain relief, anesthesia and palliative care, among others. Their schedules define the rules under which these substances are to be available for medical use in national contexts, and the provisions countries put in place to avoid their diversion to the illegal market. As such, scheduling (classification)[12] of these substances in the tables of the conventions is one of the main functions of the drug control regime. It is also the hardest balance to achieve between availability for medical use and prohibition of non-medical use.

The scheduling of psychoactive substances is a process designed to effectively balance this prevention of abuse with the availability of substances for medical and scientific use. This process, operating at both international and national levels, is set to enable coordinated efforts among law enforcement, justice, and health services, and is highly codified. At the international level, scheduling procedures can be initiated by states parties under the 1961 and 1971 Conventions or the World Health Organization (WHO), and the INCB for the 1988 Convention. Substance assessments focus on their abuse potential, health risks, and therapeutic value. The WHO's Expert Committee on Drug Dependence (ECDD) evaluates substances under the 1961 and 1971 Conventions and recommends scheduling levels to the Commission on Narcotic Drugs (CND). The INCB conducts assessments under the 1988 Convention. The CND decides the scheduling of substances, which then trickles down to national legal frameworks. The substances are categorized into schedules based on their abuse potential, health risks, and medical utility (more details in the next section).

Under the 1961 Convention, substances are classified into four schedules, with Schedules I and II indicating the highest control levels based on the balance between abuse potential and medical usefulness. Schedule I substances have high abuse potential and limited medical use, while Schedule II substances are more widely used in medicine with lower abuse liability. Schedules III and IV address drug preparations for legitimate medical use and substances with particularly dangerous properties, respectively. The 1971 Convention introduces a sliding scale to categorize substances into four schedules based on their therapeutic usefulness and abuse risk. Schedule I contains substances with high abuse risk and low therapeutic value, while Schedule IV includes those with lower abuse risk and higher therapeutic utility. The 1988 Convention focuses on precursor chemicals, categorized into Tables I and II based on their role in the illicit drug trade and their legitimate use.[13]

Nevertheless, the international scheduling system experiences some inconsistencies. One of the key inconsistencies is the division of responsibility between WHO and the INCB. This partition has led to regulatory gaps and political influences in scheduling decisions, as WHO recommendations are often subject to political negotiations within the CND. Additionally, the 1988 Convention only covers precursors for psychotropic substances, whereas precursors for narcotic drugs were already included under the 1961 Convention. This distinction has created an administrative divide in how different types of substances and their precursors are regulated, sometimes leading to inefficiencies in law enforcement efforts against illicit drug production.[14]

The international drug control regime has undergone significant evolutions, with each treaty reflecting the prevailing geopolitical, economic, and scientific considerations of its time. While the 1961 Convention consolidated earlier agreements into a unified framework, the 1971 Convention adapted to emerging synthetic drugs, and the 1988 Convention introduced an expanded focus on drug-related criminal activity. Nevertheless, they are facing massive challenges including new synthetic substances that beat the pace of scheduling and introduce new modes of production, new trafficking routes, and modes of consumption, leading to public health crises (see Chapter 2).

## CND, INCB, UNODC, and WHO: The Legislative, the Judiciary, the Executive, and the Advisory Branches of International Drug Control

The international drug control regime operates under the framework of the United Nations, with the implementation of treaties entrusted to three primary entities: (1) the Commission on Narcotic Drugs (CND), (2) the International Narcotics Control Board (INCB), (3) and the United Nations Office on Drugs and Crime (UNODC). The evaluation of substances to be classified as illegal drugs is entrusted to WHO. These bodies oversee the regulation of controlled substances, policy formulation, and data collection to implement global drug control efforts.

The CND serves as the principal political body of international drug control and can be compared to the international legislative body of drug control. Established in 1946 as a subsidiary commission of the United Nations

Economic and Social Council (ECOSOC), its mandate includes supervising treaty implementation and advising on drug-related policy. The Commission consists of 53 member states, which convene annually at the UN in Vienna to assess global drug trends, discuss policy approaches, and formulate international guidelines. The CND has significant normative functions, including revising treaty-related issues, monitoring treaty operations, and issuing policy recommendations. It also has the authority to schedule new substances or modify the scheduling of narcotic and psychotropic substances based on WHO recommendations and to adjust precursor chemical lists following INCB advice.

Since 1991, the Commission has additionally functioned as the governing body of the then newly established United Nations International Drug Control Programme (UNDCP), which later merged with a crime prevention program into UNODC.[15] Despite its role in shaping international drug policy, the CND has faced criticism regarding the composition of its delegates (traditionally from law enforcement agencies), its decision-making processes, and its reluctance to engage with contentious policy issues such as human rights and harm reduction.[16] The Commission's reliance on a long-standing (although currently disputed) consensus-based decision-making, commonly referred to as the Vienna consensus, resulted in noncommittal resolutions based on the lowest common denominator, as dissent from a single government could obstruct policy adoption.[17] Furthermore, influential states such as the United States, China, and the Russian Federation have historically dominated in drug policy discussions. It was not until the early 2010s that dissent came from Latin American countries requesting a UN General Assembly Special Session on drugs to address the limitations of international drug policy, supported by select European countries in their struggle to upset the Vienna consensus status quo (detailed in Chapter 3).[18]

With limited judiciary powers, the INCB, an independent quasi-judicial monitoring body, was established in 1968 through the 1961 Single Convention on Narcotic Drugs. It is responsible for overseeing the application of UN drug control conventions, a role inherited from predecessor committees dating back to the League of Nations era (PCOB and DSB, see above in the treaties section). The Board comprises 13 members elected by ECOSOC, with three selected from WHO-nominated candidates with "medical, pharmacological or pharmaceutical experience," and the remaining ten from government-proposed candidates (1961 Convention, Article 9).

The INCB's responsibilities are categorized into two key areas. First, it ensures the legitimate provision of controlled substances for medical and scientific use while preventing their diversion into illicit channels. This includes monitoring states' control over precursor chemicals used in illicit drug production and evaluating weaknesses in national and international drug control frameworks, offering corrective recommendations. Secondly, it determines and controls which precursor chemicals should be subjected to international regulations (read the section on scheduling above). The Board manages a system of estimates to balance supply and demand for controlled substances and works with governments to prevent the illicit diversion of chemicals.[19] For example, to order controlled substances (e.g., morphine) countries submit an annual estimate to the INCB, which then approves it and allows them to import or produce the substance in the agreed-upon quantities. In its oversight role, the INCB maintains direct engagement with governments, requesting clarifications in cases of potential treaty violations (such as the recent legalization of non-medical cannabis in Canada or Uruguay), suggesting corrective actions, and assisting with implementation challenges. If a serious breach occurs and remedial measures are insufficient, the Board may take the matter to the CND and ECOSOC. The INCB's monitoring of legal (mainly medical) drug markets is widely respected for its accuracy. However, its role in addressing illicit drug markets has drawn criticism, with some governments and civil society organizations questioning its simple approach to complex policy debates, with a blind push for prohibition despite the multifaceted drug-related situations in regional and national contexts.[20]

WHO, as the entity in charge of health across the UN system, is mandated by the drug conventions to conduct scientific evaluation of the therapeutic benefits or health threats of substances, and to determine whether they should be scheduled or not and at which level. At a governmental level, the role of WHO in the international drug control regime can be paralleled to that of an advisory constitutional body.

The 1961 Single Convention on Narcotic Drugs and the Convention on Psychotropic Substances of 1971 give WHO the mandate to assess substances to evaluate if they need to be scheduled under the international drug control regime in Article 3 of the 1961 Convention and Article 2 of the 1971 Convention. The WHO ECDD meets every year to review the literature on substances that are considered for scheduling or exemption by parties to the Conventions or by WHO itself. WHO subsequently sends the results of its review of the substances to the CND (through its Director-General and the UN Secretary-General), which takes a decision on scheduling, tables a resolution, and usually adopts the scheduling recommendations of the ECDD.

The ECDD's procedure includes the priority for public health protection and ensuring the availability and access to scheduled substances for scientific and medical reasons. The ECDD bases its reviews on evidence, within the mandate given to it by the Conventions and other legal instruments such as resolutions.[21] The ECDD made headlines in December 2020 when the CND voted in favor of its recommendation to de-schedule cannabis and cannabis resin from Schedule IV of the Single Convention on Narcotic Drugs of 1961,[22] thus allowing countries to legally implement medical cannabis programs nationally, with strict control against diversion to the illegal market. This vote received media attention in several parts of the world as a liberalization of cannabis, when it was a limited vote that did not change the international and national controls around cannabis use, and still strictly prohibits its non-medical use. Currently, the ECDD is reviewing the scheduling of the coca leaf, following an exemption request introduced by Bolivia in 2023.[23]

Probably the one with the least characteristics of an executive body, since its role is limited to technical assistance, data collection, and support for legislative changes to implement the conventions, UNODC serves as the technical body of the international drug control regime. Established through the merger of the UNDCP and the Centre for International Crime Prevention, the Office oversees UN initiatives related to drug control. It is unique in the UN system as it has two governing bodies, and other than the CND, the Commission on Crime Prevention and Criminal Justice (CCPCJ) oversees crime prevention and counterterrorism. UNODC is not mandated any role by the three drug conventions, contrary to the three above-mentioned bodies, since no specific entity on drugs existed within the UN system during their negotiation and adoption, but it has inherited some normative functions from the UN Secretary-General, mainly regarding the process of scheduling. In drug policy, UNODC implements programs focused on prevention, treatment, rehabilitation, alternative development, and harm reduction related to HIV and hepatitis prevention, especially in prison settings. It also publishes key data reporting such as the annual World Drug Report to inform global drug control strategies. Additionally, it supports states in harmonizing their legal and criminal justice frameworks.

The international drug control regime, implemented through the UN system, is characterized by a complex interplay between political, regulatory, and technical bodies. While the INCB, CND, UNODC, and WHO each fulfill distinct roles, their operations are subject to ongoing debates concerning effectiveness, transparency, and ideological biases. Criticisms range from the INCB's perceived rigidity in addressing illicit markets to the CND's consensus-based limitations and WHO's limited input to policymaking. As drug policy reform debates intensify, these bodies face increasing scrutiny regarding their adaptability to contemporary drug-related challenges and emerging threats (more details in Chapter 2).

## Origins of the International Control Regime

The international drug control regime dates nevertheless back to the early twentieth century and the China-U.S. agreement of the 1909 Shanghai Opium Commission. It has further developed over half a century through the introduction of four different binding treaties. The first national control measures came through the opium trade in the eighteenth century in China and colonial territories in East Asia, which led colonial administrations to grant exclusive retail distribution rights to private contractors who maximized profits by promoting widespread consumption (including opium in India and coca leaf in Indonesia). In an effort to address trade imbalances, European powers expanded the opium trade to China despite the Chinese government's ban on imports in the 1790s. During the nineteenth century, European powers used war and coercive trade agreements to ensure open access to the Chinese market, which resulted in a significant increase in opium imports. The Chinese government, in response to mounting financial pressures, rescinded its ban on opium to generate tax revenue, allowing domestic cultivators to enter the business.[24] The origins of international drug control are deeply tied to the legacy of the Opium Wars (1839–1842, 1856–1860), which forced China to accept the opium trade under British pressure. These wars resulted in the Treaty of Nanjing (1842) and the Treaty of Tianjin (1858), which legalized opium imports, deepening China's social and economic instability with an unprecedented flood of opium into the market.

The early twentieth century saw the emergence of the first international drug control efforts, with China playing a central role despite its political instability. It is notable that these control efforts, before the UN-era treaties, focused heavily and almost solely on reducing supply through regulation of trade and prohibition of certain uses.[25] The 1906 Britain-China "Ten Year Agreement" was a landmark bilateral effort in which China committed to eliminating domestic opium cultivation by 1918, while Britain agreed to phase out Indian opium exports. However, Britain secured the right to inspect Chinese compliance, reflecting the power imbalance between the two nations.[26] China also took broader steps toward drug control, issuing regulations on refined drugs in 1909 and 1910 and hosting the Shanghai Opium Commission in 1909,[27] widely recognized as the start of the international drug control system. Yet, the collapse of the Qing Dynasty in 1911 and the transition to the Republican era in 1912 saw the further spread of drug use due to political turmoil, allowing opium production to resume as warlords relied on the trade for revenue.[28]

At the same time, the 1912 International Opium Convention, negotiated at The Hague, was the first binding multilateral attempt to address the increasingly globalized opium trade.[29] It emerged from a patchwork of prior bilateral agreements and years of diplomatic lobbying, especially by the United States and China, frustrated by the human and economic costs of opium use and trade.[30] The treaty focused primarily on controlling the international movement of narcotics: states pledged not to export opium or its derivatives without import authorizations from recipient governments. Yet internally, governments retained wide discretion. The treaty articulated the principle of restricting drug use to medical and legitimate purposes but included no deadlines or enforcement tools. Most crucially, the Convention made no effort to regulate opium cultivation, often the economic lifeline of colonial territories, or to harmonize domestic laws. Its impact was muted by its limited scope and the reluctance of powerful states to curb practices that sustained their own strategic or economic interests.[31] China, still fragmented and weak, was left with the task of reforming while its treaty partners continued to profit from the drug trade.

The 1925 Geneva International Opium Convention represented an incremental but structurally significant evolution.[32] Negotiated under the auspices of the League of Nations, it introduced the first international system for statistical reporting on drug production, trade, and consumption. Governments were now expected to submit annual estimates of their legitimate needs and provide import/export data to a new oversight body, the PCOB, discussed in the section above. This marked a shift toward institutionalization: a bureaucratic infrastructure designed to surveil and constrain global drug flows. However, the core contradictions persisted. Colonial powers resisted curbs on opium smoking in Asia, pharmaceutical manufacturing countries, particularly Germany, demanded leniency on synthetic opioids like morphine and heroin, and military authorities secured exemptions for strategic reserves.[33] Many of the treaty's provisions remained voluntary or subject to flexible interpretation. Nevertheless, the 1925 treaty consolidated the idea that narcotics were a matter of international governance and not merely national discretion, a foundational shift, even if the mechanisms remained weak and the motivations uneven. The structure of estimates, reporting, and institutional review persists to this day under the mandate of the INCB.

The 1931 Convention for limiting the Manufacture and regulating the Distribution of Narcotic Drugs, negotiated in Geneva under the League of Nations, marked a turning point in the bureaucratization of global drug control. Unlike its predecessors, which merely encouraged states to restrain the trade and consumption of narcotics, the 1931 treaty imposed quantitative limits on manufacture, a more intrusive and technically demanding form of regulation. States were now obliged to submit advance estimates of the amounts they planned to produce, accounting for medical and scientific needs, export commitments, and reserve stocks. The treaty's architecture acknowledged the need for state-level capacity. Article 15 required each country to establish a "special administration" tasked with overseeing domestic compliance and coordinating efforts against illicit traffic. New institutions were layered into the regime. The DSB (the second predecessor of the INCB), an innovation of this treaty, was tasked with reviewing national estimates, and could even generate figures for non-participating countries, an early gesture toward universality. The PCOB saw its mandate expanded, gaining authority to monitor adherence more comprehensively. Enforcement, however, remained symbolic. These bodies could identify anomalies and publish infractions, but not impose penalties.[34]

Reflecting growing concern over trafficking networks, the treaty also introduced unprecedented requirements for international enforcement cooperation. Article 23 compelled states to collect and share detailed intelligence on seizures, smuggling routes, transport methods, and the identity of involved firms and individuals.[35] In short, it was a pivot from principle to practice, from generalized commitments to data-driven governance. Still, the 1931 Convention was far from airtight. While it imposed manufacturing limits, those estimates could be revised without consequence. Firms were not obligated to disclose the origins of their raw materials. And despite the formal apparatus for surveillance, major producers of narcotic substances retained strategic flexibility. Even with clearer rules and a more structured regime, economic interests and national sovereignty continued to constrain the effectiveness of international control.

By the second half of the 1930s, the international drug control regime had reached its technical peak in one narrow domain. Governments submitted annual estimates of narcotic requirements, compiled statistics on production, trade, and stocks, and adhered to the procedural expectations of the 1925 and 1931 treaties. The machinery functioned. The PCOB reviewed data; the DSB adjusted projections. Legitimate pharmaceutical firms, preferring predictable regulation to chaotic enforcement, complied. Diversions from licit supply chains became statistically negligible. This remains, almost a century later, one of the few uncontested successes of the system.[36]

As William McAllister reminds us, regulating pharmaceutical-grade morphine is not the same as controlling heroin on city streets. The illicit trade, not surprisingly, proved immune to forms and reporting schedules. Unlicensed manufacture continued unabated in regions where central authority was weak, corrupt, or uninterested. East Asia was especially illustrative. Japanese military expansion into China did more than undermine drug control; it normalized the drug trade as a fiscal strategy. All major actors, Japanese occupiers, Chinese nationalists, warlords resorted to narcotics trafficking to finance operations.[37] The idea that Geneva-based bureaucrats could meaningfully intervene in this environment is, with hindsight, difficult to credit. The colonial powers also undermined enforcement efforts. Colonial administrations continued to operate opium monopolies across Asia, generating state revenue while ostensibly supporting prohibition. These monopolies ensured a permanent leakage into the illicit market. Calls for abolition were dismissed as naive, both politically and economically. In effect, the system preserved a contradiction: it sought to eliminate trafficking while tolerating large-scale, state-managed production and sale.[38]

A solution was proposed in the Geneva 1936 Convention for the Suppression of the Illicit Traffic in Dangerous Drugs. It aimed to criminalize trafficking, harmonize penalties, and expand extradition. For once, the language was direct. States were expected to impose severe punishment, including imprisonment, for trafficking and related activities. The Convention even allowed for prosecuting preparatory acts, a level of foresight rare in international law at the time.[39] Yet the outcome was predictable. The treaty attracted few signatories. Legal traditions clashed, particularly over extradition and territorial jurisdiction. Major powers hesitated, especially as they needed to ensure sufficient supply of essential medicines and pain relief ahead of the war.[40]

The League of Nations-based international drug control law (the 1912 Hague Convention entered in force in 1919, followed by the 1925 Geneva Opium Convention, the 1931 Limitation Convention, and the 1936 Convention for the Suppression of the Illicit Traffic) represents a slow, incremental process of institutionalizing drug control. Each treaty expanded the international framework, first regulating the licit supply of narcotics and progressively moving toward addressing illicit production and trafficking. The early conventions were primarily concerned with restricting the manufacture and trade of opiates and other narcotics to quantities estimated as necessary for medical purposes, a clear precursor to the principle of supply reduction that would dominate later efforts. It was not until the 1936 Convention that a formal attempt was made to tackle the growing problem of international trafficking, signaling a recognition of the transnational nature of the issue. However, despite these efforts, the control regime remained fragmented and largely reactive, with enforcement gaps exacerbated by geopolitical and colonial realities. It was only post-World War II that these disparate efforts would be consolidated into a more global framework, setting the stage for the current drug control system.

# Chapter 2

# TENSIONS IN THE IMPLEMENTATION OF INTERNATIONAL DRUG LAWS

The international drug control regime, as constructed over the past century, operates on a foundational but empirically debatable premise that the complete elimination of non-medical drug use is achievable. Despite periodic reaffirmation of this goal, most recently through four global political declarations over the last 16 years (detailed in Chapter 3), the empirical record shows persistent growth in drug markets, widening geographic reach, and increasing consumption across all continents. The strategy of prohibition, though designed with public health and safety in mind, has generated a range of adverse structural outcomes. The UN itself, in 2008, acknowledged what it called the unintended consequences of drug control when looking into the outcomes of a century of international drug laws (since the Shanghai Opium Commission of 1909). These included the displacement of policy priorities, the militarization of enforcement, the global redistribution of drug production and violence, and the marginalization of drug consumers.[1] These are not marginal effects; they are systemic, recurrent, and measurable. The illicit drug economy, the second illicit market globally, thrives in the vacuum created by prohibition, financing organized crime and destabilizing governance structures, especially in low- and middle-income transit or producer regions.

Moreover, the rigidity of drug control law has increasingly collided with other established areas of international legal obligation, especially human rights, health, and development. Tensions arise not merely from competing goals but from institutional and legal incompatibilities. For example, international drug treaties' interpretation and implementation promoted incarceration over treatment, criminalization over harm reduction, and control over access for legitimate medical uses while certainly allowing countries to sovereignly choose the degree of severity.

This chapter explores those fault lines. It traces how the drug control framework, conceived in the early twentieth century and expanded in a piecemeal fashion, has been confronted with evolving global norms and evidence. As a result, the regime now stands as a rare example of a global legal architecture in direct tension with multiple other pillars of the international system. Understanding these contradictions is not just a matter of legal analysis, it is a prerequisite for understanding the calls for reformed policy responses in a world that is anything but drug-free.

## International Human Rights Law and Illegal Drug Supply Reduction

The global drug economy, valued conservatively between USD 426 and 652 billion (an average USD 500 billion annual turnover mostly in cash and cryptocurrency transactions),[2] represents a colossal distortion of economic incentives, one that extracts labor from the world's most precarious populations and rewards organized criminal enterprise while hollowing out legitimate development pathways. In many countries, the illicit drug trade functions as an economic fallback, an employer of last resort.[3] The correlation between economic marginality and penal severity is not coincidental; it is structural, and it undermines any serious ambition toward building equitable and sustainable societies as foreseen in Latin American countries, where drug cartels control territories, and where 39 of the 50 most violent cities in the world are found.[4] In response to this colossal illegal market, it is estimated that the financial commitments to drug law enforcement absorb approximately USD 100 billion on an annual basis (while this might be an outdated figure, the current one is certainly bigger).[5] This figure highlights a significant structural outcome that shapes both the fiscal landscape and the broader societal outcomes of drug control.

Illicit financial flows, especially those generated by the global drug trade, remain resistant to accurate measurement, and this is not merely a statistical inconvenience. It is a structural blind spot. Even in highly regulated financial environments such as Europe, Europol concedes that a staggering 98 percent of criminal proceeds go unrecovered.[6] In other words, the system that ostensibly exists to intercept and dismantle criminal financial operations functions, in practice, as a sieve. The resilience of these flows is underwritten by a familiar yet still underappreciated array of enablers. Cryptocurrencies offer pseudonymity and transnational reach; offshore financial havens insulate wealth from scrutiny; currency smuggling operates in physical space with an efficiency digital surveillance has yet to match. And overlaying all of this is institutional complicity, whether willful or negligent, among both financial intermediaries and state actors.[7] These elements are not marginal; they constitute the operational backbone of modern drugs capitalism. The result is a global economic architecture in which criminal liquidity moves faster and more freely than legitimate capital, effectively colonizing entire sectors of the formal economy. And as long as illicit financial flows remain embedded in the very structures meant to contain them, no serious policy on drug control, development, or financial transparency can be said to exist.

Moreover, corruption among state actors and the erosion of institutional integrity are pivotal in facilitating the flow of illicit drugs. Criminal organizations exploit their connections to corrupt officials, enabling them to operate with impunity, transporting consignments without fear of detection or interception, utilizing established infrastructure, and benefiting from protection against prosecution.[8] Drug trafficking organizations also strategically aim to undermine democratic processes, particularly elections, as a means of weakening state institutions, eliminating threats to their interests, and embedding corrupt and criminal elements within governance.[9] The unprecedented scale of violence during Mexico's 2024 elections underscored this dynamic starkly, with 37 political candidates murdered in the lead-up to the elections (at least 28 linked to organized crime), resulting in numerous withdrawals due to intimidation.[10]

The tough state responses to the grim picture of the illegal drug market directly resulted in over-incarceration and prison overcrowding. Roughly 2.5 million people are incarcerated worldwide for drug-related offenses, about one in every five prisoners, making drug offenses the main purveyor of prison population globally. Of those, an estimated 60 percent are behind bars for drug possession, and only 20 percent on charges for drug trafficking.[11] This outcome, when assessed through the lens of policy efficiency and resource allocation, reflects a striking misalignment between stated goals and measurable outcomes. Despite decades of enforcement rhetoric focused on dismantling transnational criminal networks, the machinery of drug control appears more focused on the least powerful actors, mainly individuals with minimal involvement in large-scale trafficking.

Drug offenses remain punishable by death in no fewer than 35 countries and territories, a legal relic that persists despite mounting evidence of its inefficacy and disproportionate application. In 2024, more than 600 people were executed for drug-related crimes, with more than 2,300 people on death row currently.[12] Such figures underscore the uncomfortable truth that in significant portions of the world, capital punishment continues to operate not as a last resort for the most egregious crimes, but as a routine instrument of drug policy. Executing individuals for drug crimes does not eliminate supply chains, dismantle trafficking networks, or resolve the demand for drugs. The application of the death penalty as a deterrent to drug trafficking, production, and sale remains highly contentious, facing strong opposition from international human rights bodies and drug control organizations.[13] The

International Covenant on Civil and Political Rights, through Article 6, restricts the use of capital punishment in countries where it has not been abolished, confining it to the most serious crimes, those in which the taking of life is intentional. Drug-related offenses, therefore, fall outside the scope of this exception.[14] Worse, the actions of Philippine President Rodrigo Duterte (currently arrested by the ICC on indirect co-perpetrator for the crime against humanity of murder charges)[15] starkly illustrate human rights violations, as his reinvigorated war on drugs has led to a surge of extrajudicial killings of thousands of people.[16] These acts, carried out by both state actors and vigilante groups, underscore the devastating consequences of a policy that prioritizes violent enforcement over human rights and due process.

At the international level, human rights mandates that were silent on drug control laws for years have fully engaged in drug policy governance in the last 15 years. In March 2015, the Human Rights Council (HRC) adopted its first-ever resolution on drug policy as a contribution to the 2016 United Nations General Assembly Special Session (UNGASS) on the world drug problem. This resolution led to the production of the first-ever report by the High Commissioner for Human Rights on the impact of drug control policies on human rights.[17] The resolution reflected growing concerns about human rights violations under drug control, an issue that had been raised by the HRC, the High Commissioner for Human Rights, and its Special Procedures.

Between 2010 and 2024, the HRC Special Procedures were among the most vocal opponents to current drug control, highlighting the tensions between international human rights and drug laws. The Special Rapporteurs on Torture expressed alarm over the growing practice of governments derogating from the prohibition of torture, particularly under the pretext of exceptional security measures, with drug offenses frequently cited among the justifications;[18] the UN Special Rapporteur on the right to health criticized the international drug control system, asserting its failure to account for the realities of drug use and addiction, exacerbating public health outcomes; and the significant barriers to accessing essential medicines, including pain relief and substitution therapy, in many countries;[19] the Special Rapporteur on Violence against Women reported widespread human rights violations against women related to drug policies, including coercion into drug smuggling and incarceration for drug offenses linked to relationships, a phenomenon known as the "girlfriend problem";[20] the Working Group on Arbitrary Detention advocated for the decriminalization of drug use and possession, the prioritization of non-custodial alternatives for minor offenses, and a review of arrest and detention procedures;[21] the Working Group of Experts on People of African Descent called the war on drugs a form of racial control disproportionately affecting people of color;[22] and the Special Rapporteur on

Extrajudicial Executions condemned the alleged extrajudicial executions of people who use drugs and dealers in the Philippines.[23]

Following the adoption of the resolution on the HRC's contribution to UNGASS, a group of governments introduced a resolution in 2018 to ensure the Council's involvement in the implementation of the UNGASS Outcome Document. A third resolution was adopted in 2023 requesting the High Commissioner to produce a new report. The High Commissioner called for countries to review the usefulness of the legal regulation of all drugs, being the first UN mandate holder ever to question the prohibition and elimination of drugs at the core of the drug conventions, and thus going directly against the international drug control regime.[24] The High Commissioner for Human Rights consistently advocated for the protection of human rights within the context of drug control, emphasizing that individuals do not forfeit their human rights by using drugs, including access to health, life, freedom from arbitrary arrest, and protection from torture.

## Global Health Obligations and Challenges

WHO (the World Health Organization), as the designated authority on health within the multilateral system, plays a central role in shaping global health policy, including in areas that intersect with drug control. The stated objective of the international drug control regime is the promotion of "the health and welfare of (hu)mankind."[25] However, the punitive framework through which drug control is implemented, especially the criminalization of consumption, has introduced measurable public health consequences, particularly among populations that use drugs. WHO's constitutional definition of health as encompassing physical, mental, and social well-being[26] positions the organization in direct engagement with the health implications of drug control policies.[27] This section focuses on the normative functions of WHO, beyond its drug treaty-mandated role described in Chapter 1 and in the following section on access to controlled medicines.

One of the most extensively documented intersections between drug control and health outcomes concerns the spread of HIV among people who inject drugs (PWID). WHO, alongside UNODC and UNAIDS (Joint UN Program on HIV/AIDS), has developed evidence-based harm reduction guidelines, which include needle and syringe programs, opioid substitution therapy, and antiretroviral treatment.[28] These interventions were endorsed by governments at ECOSOC, the CND, and the UNAIDS Program Coordinating Board, reflecting international consensus on their effectiveness in reducing HIV transmission. Yet, despite this institutional approval, implementation remains inconsistent, primarily due to political resistance and resource allocation priorities. WHO's Global Health Sector Strategy on HIV/AIDS 2022–2030 called for scaled-up harm reduction programs and the development of services tailored to stimulant users,[29] yet progress remains uneven across regions.

The epidemiological data illustrate the extent of the challenge. While global HIV infections have been decreasing, HIV prevalence among PWID globally stood at a median of 5 percent (in 2022), a figure seven times higher than that observed in the general adult population.[30] In Eastern Europe and Central Asia, where harm reduction services are often restricted, PWID account for up to 27 percent of new HIV infections.[31] As of the latest estimates, globally, PWID face a fourteenfold higher risk of acquiring HIV compared to the general population. In 2022, approximately one in eight individuals in this group, an estimated 1.6 million people, were living with HIV,[32] making this demographic one of the most vulnerable to co-infections such as hepatitis and tuberculosis.

The 2021–2026 political declaration on HIV/AIDS, the shared global commitment adopted at the UN General Assembly every five years, calls for the elimination of discrimination in access to harm reduction services and the adoption of interventions outlined in technical guidance from UNAIDS, WHO, and UNODC to prevent HIV transmission among PWID.[33] A decade earlier, the 2011 declaration set a target of reducing HIV transmission among this population by 50 percent by 2015. However, by 2013, UNAIDS reported that the reduction had reached only 10 percent, well below the stated objective.[34] The main driver of this epidemic among PWID is the global lack of harm reduction services. There is no evidence to suggest that harm reduction programs encourage drug injection or undermine policies aimed at reducing demand and supply. On the contrary, opioid substitution therapy and methadone programs have been shown to reduce opioid dependence, lower injection-related risk behaviors, prevent HIV transmission, and improve adherence to antiretroviral treatment among PWID living with HIV.[35] Furthermore, WHO's guidelines on opioid dependence treatment emphasize the efficacy of opioid agonist therapy. These treatments reduce heroin use, overdose risks, and drug-related crime. WHO maintains that opioid withdrawal programs have poor long-term outcomes compared to maintenance therapies and should only be pursued when preferred by the individual.[36] Other HIV prevention strategies, such as pre-exposure prophylaxis (PrEP) and treatment as prevention (TasP), have not yet been systematically evaluated for this population.[37] Western Europe has implemented extensive harm reduction measures, reducing HIV transmission in this population to approximately 1 percent. In Switzerland, annual new infections in PWID dropped from over 900 people in the late 1980s to four (a reported three men and one woman) by 2023.[38]

A lingering issue that has every chance of aggravating in the coming years is related to the funding of these harm reduction services, especially since they depend on international aid and that major European and the United States have decided on massive cuts to their aid starting in 2025. UNAIDS estimated that USD 2.3 billion would be required in 2015, decreasing to USD 1.5 billion in 2020, for an effective response to HIV among PWID in low- and middle-income countries.[39] Yet, only 6 percent of this need is met, with just USD 131 million allocated, down from 10 percent coverage a decade earlier. Only 0.7 percent of global HIV funding goes to harm reduction services.[40]

Another issue is the lack of availability, and at scale, of these services. Among the 158 countries reporting drug use, 108 have incorporated harm reduction into their policies. Around 93 offer needle and syringe programs, while 94 have opioid agonist programs (mainly time and scope limited pilots).[41] Furthermore, less than 1 percent of PWID live in countries where their harm reduction needs are fully met,[42] and where HIV and other blood-borne diseases' transmission can be effectively prevented.

Beyond HIV, hepatitis C represents another significant health burden among PWID. Of the estimated 14 million PWID worldwide, approximately 6.8 million (an estimated one in two people) are living with hepatitis C, making them the population concerned with nearly a quarter of all new infections globally.[43] Although effective treatments for hepatitis C exist, their availability remains constrained by cost barriers, stigma, and exclusionary treatment policies that limit access for PWID. Exclusion from government-funded hepatitis C treatment in many parts of the world is often justified by concerns over reinfection risk and doubts about adherence to therapy among PWID.[44] However, WHO's guidelines make clear that such reasoning is misguided. Evidence shows that providing treatment to this population is not only cost-effective but also essential for reducing transmission and lowering overall prevalence.[45] In May 2014, the World Health Assembly adopted its first resolution on hepatitis. It urged governments to implement harm reduction measures developed by WHO, UNODC, and UNAIDS, to guarantee equitable access to health services for high-risk populations, and to re-examine policies that discriminate against people with hepatitis.[46] A comparable resolution followed at the CND in March 2017, when UN member states passed a resolution focused on the prevention of hepatitis among PWID. It called for access to hepatitis C treatment, application of the harm reduction framework to curb new infections, and alignment of national legislation with international standards.[47] Despite these governance efforts and evidence, entrenched policies and stigma continue to hinder access on the ground, undermining broader public health efforts.

Drug use accounts for approximately 1 percent of all disability-adjusted life years (DALYs), a metric that incorporates both premature mortality and years of life lived with disability due to conditions such as suicide, overdose, AIDS, and hepatitis.[48] People with a drug use disorder, who represent 22 percent of the global population of people who use drugs, experience significantly higher mortality rates compared to the general population. The largest share of drug-attributable DALYs is found in drug use disorders, followed by cirrhosis linked to chronic hepatitis C from injecting drug use, HIV, and cancers: "Drug-attributable DALYs were highest for drug use disorders (20.4 million DALYs, 95% UI 16.2–24.7), cancers (1.6 million DALYs, 1.4–1.9) and cirrhosis (4.8 million DALYs, 4.2–5.5) driven by chronic hepatitis C infection due to injecting drug use, and HIV (3.2 million DALYs, 2.6–3.9). There were similar patterns for deaths, YLLs, and YLDs. Overall, 452,000 deaths (420,000–487,000) were attributed to drug use."[49]

The overdose epidemic in the United States and Canada, reported and aggravating since 2012, has shed light on the high mortality of potent opioids and stimulants, and the difficulty of reducing overdose death rates even in countries with good health surveillance mechanisms, effective and modern health systems, and financial capacity to address this crisis. In the United States, drug overdose deaths exceeded a staggering 107,000 in 2023. These fatalities, largely fentanyl-related (with over 74,000 deaths by this synthetic opioid alone) underscore the persistence of a crisis now well into its second decade. In 2020, approximately 1.7 million individuals received treatment for substance use disorders in the United States. Of these, 282,000 were identified as using non-prescribed pharmaceutical products, while 93,000 reported the use of solvents and inhalants. National prevalence figures reveal that 4.43 percent of the population used opioids in some form, with 3.66 percent specifically using prescription opioids. The reported use of tranquilizers and sedatives stood at 2.09 percent, and amphetamines at 1.10 percent.[50] Meanwhile, enforcement efforts have intensified. In 2023, the Drug Enforcement Administration (DEA) seized more than 77 million fentanyl tablets and nearly 12,000 pounds of powdered fentanyl, an unprecedented volume in the agency's history. Yet the scale of seizure data must be read not only as a measure of control but also as an indirect indicator of availability and circulation. Fentanyl has become the focal point of U.S. drug policy enforcement.[51] In 2023, fentanyl was implicated in 16.3 percent of all federal drug trafficking cases, an increase of over 244.7 percent since 2019. Trafficking cases involving fentanyl analogues, although smaller in absolute number (1.4 percent in 2024), have also increased by more than 113.5 percent over the same period.[52]

Despite these substantial health burdens, effective and inexpensive harm reduction interventions are at hand. Naloxone, an opioid antagonist medication, is a cost-effective tool for reversing opioid overdoses, and its inclusion in national drug policies has been recommended since 2012. The WHO and UNODC's joint "Stop Overdose Safely" initiative aims to expand training for health and social workers and scale up harm reduction services in national health systems.[53] Since 2021, under the Biden-Harris administration, the federal government has for the first time acknowledged harm reduction as a legitimate pillar of drug policy, complementing existing approaches focused on supply suppression and treatment. This represents a notable deviation from previous federal frameworks, which had largely confined harm reduction measures to local or state jurisdictions.[54] And after more than a decade of increasingly sustained mortality, the opioid crisis appears to have entered a period of partial attenuation. According to provisional data from the Centers for Disease Control and Prevention (CDC), the number of drug overdose deaths declined by 12.7 percent between May 2023 and May 2024.[55] This recent downturn has been tentatively attributed to several interacting variables. One is a measurable decline in the purity of illicit fentanyl, now frequently adulterated with compounds such as BTMPS, an industrial stabilizer typically used to prevent UV degradation in plastics. While toxic, BTMPS lacks the acute lethality of high-purity fentanyl.[56] Another possible factor is demographic attrition. Years of elevated overdose mortality may have effectively reduced the size of the user population, a dynamic some have termed "exhausted user base."[57]

The last area where tensions are high between drug control laws and public health I would like to focus on is in humanitarian settings, an area highly neglected by existing literature. Most that exists focuses on drug use within refugee camps. By mid-2024, the United Nations High Commissioner for Refugees (UNHCR) was overseeing the conditions of 32 million displaced individuals globally, encompassing formal camps, informal settlements, and transitional shelters. In parallel, the United Nations Relief and Works Agency for Palestine Refugees in the Near East (UNRWA) administered services to more than 5.8 million people, primarily in protracted refugee situations across the Middle East. These populations face multiple layers of vulnerability, and those engaged in illicit or non-medical drug use are among the most marginalized. The use of psychoactive substances often increases in the context of forced displacement, not necessarily as a cultural artifact, but as a coping mechanism against sustained psychological stress, social dislocation, and physical precarity. In many cases, initiation into drug use occurs in the camp setting itself.[58]

For displaced individuals with a history of drug dependence, forced interruptions to existing harm reduction or substitution treatment programs, frequent in emergency settings, carry immediate health risks and wider implications for camp dynamics. Yet the provision of these services remains limited to nonexistent across most humanitarian contexts.[59] The structural inadequacy of the response is not due to the idiosyncrasies of a particular camp, but rather to the widespread institutional reluctance to address drug use among refugees with evidence-based policies.

Empirical evidence, although limited, supports this conclusion. A study conducted by UNODC across 18 Afghan refugee camps in Pakistan's North-West Frontier Province estimated the prevalence of illicit drug use at 2.6 percent. However, the report emphasized this is a conservative figure: cultural practices such as oral opium use, particularly among women and children, are underreported. When including both licit and illicit substances, usage rates in the camps surpass 15 percent.[60] In the nearby urban center of Peshawar, 8 percent of PWID were identified as Afghan refugees, further pointing to a systemic spillover from camp settings into urban health networks.[61]

In the Palestinian camps of Lebanon, which house roughly half of the country's 452,000 registered refugees, a different pattern has emerged. These camps, largely outside Lebanese regulatory frameworks, have seen a rise in the diversion of controlled prescription drugs for recreational use. Access to medications like Tramadol (a synthetic opioid) and Xanax (a benzodiazepine) is made easier by loosely regulated pharmacies and the absence of effective oversight. Legal constraints prevent Palestinian refugees from acquiring Lebanese citizenship or entering many formal professions, further compounding socio-economic marginalization and limiting access to proper healthcare.[62]

UNHCR has begun, in the last 15 years and despite its repetitive funding crunches, to address these intersecting crises. In collaboration with WHO, it has developed an assessment tool for substance use in humanitarian settings, recognizing that the primary risks include overdose, severe withdrawal symptoms, and the spread of blood-borne diseases in the absence of harm reduction services. A separate framework developed with UNAIDS aims to measure HIV vulnerabilities specifically among PWID in displaced populations. Nevertheless, current efforts remain partial and under-institutionalized. UNHCR's mandate, rooted in the 1951 Refugee Convention and the Universal Declaration of Human Rights, grants it the legitimacy to engage more robustly with the health and social unintended and negative consequences of current drug control policies. While unlikely any time soon, a revisit of the refugee operational frameworks and integration of drug policy concerns into broader humanitarian strategies, particularly in contexts of displacement, conflict, and post-conflict recovery, would be welcome to lift the burden on the most marginalized and reduce the gap between the aims of international drug control law and its unintended consequences.

Overall, the interaction between drug control policies and global health objectives reflects a broader tension between security-driven frameworks and public health imperatives, even if drug international law and its conventions provide sufficient leeway to countries to implement services, such is the case in Europe. While international agreements recognize the need for harm reduction services to address overdose deaths, HIV and hepatitis C transmission, established evidence supports intervention strategies that remain underfunded and politically contentious. The persistence of these gaps suggests that policy decisions and international implementation are driven less by empirical assessments of effectiveness and more by entrenched institutional and political constraints. The underlying issue is not a lack of knowledge, but the inertia of existing regulatory structures. This further strengthens the defiance toward the three drug conventions and adds to the list of unintended consequences of the international drug control regime's implementation.

## The Difficult Case of Access to Controlled Medicines

Among the many unintended consequences of international drug law compliance, access to medicines scheduled under the drug conventions and essential for pain relief or anesthesia is, in my opinion, and by far the worst case at hand. International drug law was designed and ratified on the premise and promise of simultaneously banning non-medical use and promoting access to psychoactive substances for medical use and research purposes. Nevertheless, the last 60 years of implementation of drug laws have resulted in a strong emphasis on prohibition of recreational use and an almost neglect of legitimate medical use. The international drug control regime entrusts WHO with the task of assessing whether specific substances merit international scheduling. This responsibility, codified in Article 3 of the 1961 Convention and Article 2 of the 1971 Convention, has been executed for decades by WHO's ECDD. Meeting annually, the ECDD reviews scientific and clinical data submitted by WHO itself or by treaty parties and formulates recommendations for the scheduling or exemption of substances. These assessments are transmitted to the CND, which typically endorses the ECDD's conclusions and formalizes them through resolutions (more details in Chapter 1).

The ECDD's mandate is anchored in public health priorities while balancing the legal obligation to ensure the availability of controlled substances for medical and scientific use. Its reviews are evidence-based and shaped by treaty obligations and relevant resolutions. Since its inception, the committee has evaluated more than 450 substances. Between WHO's establishment in 1948 and now, international scheduling expanded to include 141 narcotics and over 150 psychotropic substances.[63] However, the emergence of new psychoactive substances (NPS) presents a challenge that the current process is not well-equipped to address, with over 40 new NPS appearing annually, the ECDD's once-yearly meeting and limited capacity constrain its responsiveness, and with it the efficacy and capacity of international drug law. This also affects the level of availability, accessibility, and affordability of these substances for medical use. As of now, WHO lists 12 medicines containing internationally controlled substances in its Model List of Essential Medicines. These substances, which include drugs used in palliative care, anesthesia, mental health, and opioid dependence treatment, are indispensable to healthcare systems. Their classification under international control does not negate the obligation to ensure access, an obligation derived from both international drug treaties and human rights law.

Yet access remains deeply unequal. WHO estimates that 5.5 billion people, 83 percent of the global population, live in countries with insufficient or nonexistent access to controlled medicines.[64] These are predominantly lower-income nations, where treatment for moderate to severe pain is frequently unavailable, with "1 million end-stage HIV/AIDS patients, 5.5 million terminal cancer patients, 0.8 million patients suffering injuries, caused by accidents and violence, patients with chronic illnesses, patients recovering from surgery, women in labor (110 million births each year) as well as pediatric patients."[65] Morphine, the foundational opioid analgesic, remains profoundly underutilized in low- and middle-income countries, where only 4 percent of the global supply is distributed. The disparity is stark: while a patient in a high-income country might receive 47,600 grams of morphine, one in a low-income setting typically receives just 10 grams, if any at all.[66] Basically, one would be wise to choose in which country to get a serious injury requiring pain relief, as in most places around the world, and despite their best will, health professionals just have no training to prescribe or administer it, or simply have never seen or used it throughout their careers. The same applies to aging populations requiring palliative care.

Over the last decade, the World Health Assembly has passed several resolutions addressing these systemic failures. A resolution on cancer care emphasized the need for opioid analgesics in treatment. Another, focused on access to essential medicines, instructed states to reform procurement, pricing, and regulatory practices. In 2014, a resolution on palliative care explicitly called for the removal of legal and logistical barriers that restrict opioid access. The

2015 resolution on anesthesia went further, urging collaboration between WHO, the INCB, UNODC, and national authorities to improve access to controlled medicines necessary for surgery and emergency care.[67] At the 2016 UNGASS on the world drug problem, governments renewed their commitment to addressing barriers that prevent access to controlled medicines. This commitment encompassed legal reforms, better health infrastructure, workforce training, pricing regulation, and improvements in data collection.[68]

Nevertheless, the operational gap between formal commitment and effective implementation remains wide. Despite decades of international resolutions and repeated expressions of intent, access to controlled medicines continues to be among the most persistent tension areas between drug control obligations and public health requirements, and with devastating impacts on populations not concerned by illegal drug production, trafficking, or consumption, but with severe medical conditions requiring assistance.

## Emerging Challenges to Drug Control Laws, from Synthetic Drugs to the Dark Web Market

Beyond the UN-stated unintended consequences of international drug control, the negative outcomes discussed above on global health, access to medicines, and the criminal justice system, there are a series of emerging challenges from the appearance of potent synthetic substances on the market disrupting the scheduling system at the heart of drug control, to new trafficking routes through regions that were spared so far (such as cocaine through West Africa or heroin through eastern coasts of Africa), the rise of dark web markets and cryptocurrency payments questioning the efficiency of anti-money laundering efforts, or the legalization of cannabis for non-medical use in some U.S. states, Canada, Uruguay, Germany, Luxembourg, and others. This section will focus on two main emerging issues: the synthetic drugs market and dark web trafficking techniques.

The past decade has witnessed significant growth in the availability of synthetic drugs. However, only a limited number of these substances, particularly methamphetamine, have established global distribution networks. Methamphetamine is among the most widely used and supplied synthetic drugs worldwide, with increasing prevalence in almost every region in the world. Other synthetic drugs remain concentrated in specific regions (methamphetamine in East Asia, fentanyl and its analogues in North America, captagon in the Middle East, or synthetic stimulants in Southern Africa and Australia).

Unlike plant-based drugs, synthetic substances offer distinct logistical and financial advantages for illegal manufacturers. Production relies on precursor chemicals that are often widely available or can be substituted, while advancements in synthesis techniques enable increased yields, reduced production scale, and the development of new compounds that surpass traditional substances in potency or circumvent existing regulatory controls. The past four decades have seen rapid growth in global pharmaceutical and chemical industries, particularly in Asia. WHO estimates that China is the largest individual producer of active pharmaceutical ingredients by volume, manufacturing over 2,000 products and accounting for approximately 25 percent of global production, with annual output nearing 2 million metric tons. India follows as another major supplier.[69] The production of synthetic drugs is further facilitated by the availability of industrial equipment, including commercial-scale reaction vessels, standard laboratory glassware, and automated tableting machines. Regulatory oversight of such equipment remains limited in most countries.

Additionally, suppliers benefit from the ability to process and distribute synthetic drugs in consumer-friendly formats, such as tablets, which appeal to users who avoid injectable substances.[70] Two additional advantages of synthetic drug production include reduced manufacturing timelines and greater geographic flexibility.

Synthetic drugs often exhibit significantly higher potency than their plant-based counterparts. Fentanyl, for example, is exponentially more potent than heroin, allowing traffickers to transport smaller quantities while maintaining equivalent distribution volumes. This efficiency reduces both logistical costs and legal risks. Estimates suggest that only a few metric tons of pure fentanyl could meet the annual illicit opioid demand in the United States, whereas approximately 50 metric tons of heroin would be required to fulfill the same market demand.[71]

Jason Eligh at the Global Initiative against Transnational Organized Crime has also identified five major impacts of the synthetic drug markets that change the game of drug control and put further pressure on international drug law, as well as the need to modernize it. Two distinct opioid crises persist. The overdose epidemic in the United States and Canada is driven by high demand, while a global shortage of pain relief affects an estimated 87 percent of the world population, leading to illicit substitution and an expansion of synthetic opioid markets. Synthetic drug production is influenced by economic and logistical factors, including precursor chemical availability, access to skilled chemists, synthesis site selection, transportation infrastructure, and market accessibility. Unlike plant-based drugs, synthetic drugs can be produced in a wide range of locations. Open access to chemical knowledge, precursor alternatives, market trends, logistics, and digital resources enables the rapid evolution of synthetic drug markets. Additionally, digital platforms facilitate connections between suppliers and retail or industrial commerce networks. Increasingly complex drug formulations incorporating multiple compounds are shaping synthetic drug markets. Forensic analyses have detected the prevalence of adulterants such as xylazine in North America, nitazenes in Europe, and benzodiazepine-laced substances in various markets. Monitoring and analyzing synthetic drug markets remains a challenge, even in jurisdictions with advanced forensic capabilities. The identification of novel compounds and contaminants continues to be a significant obstacle in drug market surveillance.[72]

While synthetic drugs are unlikely to fully replace plant-based substances in the immediate future, market trends will continue to be shaped by consumer preferences, sociocultural factors, and cost considerations. Cocaine, for instance, remains more cost-effective to produce through traditional agricultural means rather than synthetic alternatives. However, over the long term, the economic and regulatory advantages of synthetic drugs may drive a strategic shift among illicit manufacturers, altering the composition of the global drug supply.

Similarly to the synthetic drugs market, the emergence of dark web marketplaces in the context of illegal drug trafficking dates back to 2011.[73] Since then, these platforms have evolved in response to law enforcement efforts, becoming a critical component of the trafficking of chemical precursors feeding the fentanyl market in North America, for example.[74] By offering anonymity to participants across the supply chain, dark web markets introduce distinct operational characteristics that require new analytical and enforcement approaches. However, current law enforcement strategies largely mirror those applied to offline drug markets, focusing on disruption rather than adaptation. Dark web markets are online platforms that facilitate the anonymous exchange of illegal goods and services, including illicit drugs and fraudulent financial instruments such as stolen credit card data. These markets are accessible only through encryption protocols like Tor, ensuring anonymity for both buyers and sellers, while transactions are typically conducted using cryptocurrencies.[75] Operationally, dark web markets function similarly to mainstream e-commerce platforms, with administrators deriving revenue from transaction commissions rather than direct involvement in illicit sales. Vendors rely on conventional postal services, using discreet packaging methods designed to evade detection by customs and border security agencies.[76]

Dark web markets are increasingly, although still marginally, altering traditional structures of illicit drug distribution by decentralizing transactions and reducing the violence associated with territorial control. This shift presents new challenges for law enforcement agencies. The first major dark web market, Silk Road, launched in 2011. Revenue for 2012 was estimated at USD

15 million, with the majority linked to drug sales. By the time the site was shut down in late 2013, its annual revenue had grown to approximately USD 100 million.[77] In October 2013, the FBI arrested Ross Ulbricht, Silk Road's creator. The operation leading to his arrest combined digital forensics, undercover transactions, and the analysis of online activity to identify Ulbricht and locate Silk Road's servers. Ulbricht was sentenced to life in prison without parole in 2015, until his pardon in early 2025 by President Donald Trump. The closure of Silk Road represented a milestone for law enforcement, but its impact was temporary. Silk Road 2.0 emerged within weeks, facing competition from new markets such as Evolution, Agora, Hydra, and Pandora. By 2014, daily sales on dark web markets reached USD 600,000, twice the peak revenue of Silk Road. More than 40 new markets launched that year, though many had short lifespans.[78]

Shortis et al. remind that following Silk Road's seizure, market operators and users adopted new security measures. Political discourse, once prominent in Silk Road forums, declined significantly. In 2014, Operation Onymous led to the closure of six dark web markets, including Silk Road 2.0. The administrator, Blake Benthall, was arrested along with several other key figures. However, the most active markets at the time, such as Evolution and Agora, remained operational, indicating that enforcement measures were only partially effective. Law enforcement tactics included exploiting weaknesses in Tor's infrastructure, techniques later revealed to have originated from research at Carnegie Mellon University. Despite these interventions, transaction volumes on dark web markets rebounded within two months, demonstrating the resilience of these platforms.[79] In 2017, coordinated law enforcement operations resulted in the shutdown of two of the largest markets: AlphaBay and Hansa. This strategy, known as Operation Mirum, marked a shift toward undermining trust among users. The FBI secretly dismantled AlphaBay without an immediate seizure notice, leading users to migrate to Hansa, which was already under Dutch police control. Law enforcement continued operating the platform, gathering intelligence on users and vendors before ultimately shutting it down. Several users received direct warnings from authorities, signaling a more targeted approach to deterrence.[80]

Since these operations, enforcement agencies have expanded their focus beyond marketplaces to include individuals and supporting financial services. The U.S. Department of Justice launched the Joint Criminal Opioid Darknet Enforcement (J-CODE) initiative in 2018, prioritizing the disruption of fentanyl distribution networks.[81] That same year, Operation Disarray resulted in over 160 interviews aimed at deterring dark web drug transactions. Other efforts targeted cryptocurrency-based laundering mechanisms, such as the closure of the BTC-E exchange and the 2019 shutdown of BestMixer, a cryptocurrency-mixing service.[82] More recent actions include Operation Dark HunTor in 2021, which led to 150 arrests, and Operation SpecTor in 2023, the largest effort to date, with 288 arrests.[83]

Despite periodic disruptions, dark web markets exhibit a high degree of adaptability, rapidly integrating new security measures in response to enforcement actions. This pattern parallels the long-standing competition between law enforcement and drug cartels in offline markets. At the international level, and while the INCB does not directly control or monitor activities on the dark web, its mandate is indirectly connected to it through the broader scope of drug trafficking. Through its monitoring functions, the INCB can identify irregularities (that countries have most certainly already figured out before reporting their data) which may eventually trace back to underground markets, including the dark web.[84]

In a broader sense, the INCB's role is to ensure that governments are properly regulating the flow of controlled substances, tracking usage statistics, and imposing regulations that prevent their diversion. Through international drug control mechanisms and its normative framework, the INCB can only advocate for strengthening cybersecurity and digital forensics, pushing countries to enhance their ability to dismantle these covert markets, to build awareness, to foster international cooperation, and to push for legislative and technological advancements that disrupt dark web trafficking. More abruptly, international law not being equipped for this emerging challenge is not of much help to countries that must handle it alone. This is mostly why, while countries and law enforcement acknowledge the distinct challenges posed by dark web markets, responses remain anchored in conventional disruption models rather than adaptive strategies. Given the role of these platforms in precursors and synthetic drugs trafficking, a reassessment of the legal responses may be necessary to address the evolving landscape.

# Chapter 3

# WHAT TO EXPECT FROM THE GLOBAL GOVERNANCE OF DRUG CONTROL IN THE FORESEEABLE FUTURE?

## Existing Legal Options to Reform the System

In 2020, the president of the INCB Cornelis P. de Joncheere, during the very formal presentation of its 2019 report made a rare and notable acknowledgment: "We do have some very fundamental issues around the conventions, that State Parties will need to start looking at. We have to recognize that the conventions were drawn up almost 60 years ago [...] and I think it is an appropriate time to look at whether those are still fit for purpose, or whether we need new alternative instruments, and alternative approaches to deal with these problems."[1] Coming from the senior official of the very body mandated to oversee the implementation of international drug control conventions, rather than from expected quarters such as human rights organizations, public health institutions, or academia, this statement marked a significant moment. It illustrates the growing recognition, even among the system's custodians, that the existing legal framework, anchored in mid-twentieth-century assumptions, may no longer be adequate to address the complexities of contemporary drug policy challenges. This observation encapsulates the broader tension examined throughout this book: the widening gap between entrenched control paradigms and evolving realities.

The calls to reform international drug policy emerge from the stark reality that its objectives have not been met, far from it. Despite decades of sustained, often militarized efforts to curb drug production, consumption, and trafficking, all three have increased since the 1964 entry into force of the Single Convention. Alongside this failure of primary goals, a series of unintended consequences, long acknowledged, even by institutional actors, have become increasingly difficult to ignore, from the scale of the illicit market, the displacement of production and enforcement across regions, to the structural entrenchment of criminal economies. More troubling still are the ripple effects, such as rising levels of violence, growing influence of organized crime, systemic human rights violations, the immense financial burden of enforcement, and recurring public health crises. These are now compounded by new challenges including synthetic drugs, online marketplaces, and technological shifts in distribution and control (as detailed in Chapter 2). Yet proponents of the regime resist the conclusion of significant shortcomings, pointing instead to one outcome, that drug-related mortality, they argue, remains comparatively low,[2] especially when contrasted with the more than 2.5 million annual deaths linked to alcohol and the 8 million attributed to tobacco.

Reform is not easy. The prohibition of narcotic drugs and psychotropic substances for non-medical or scientific purposes is a given, entrenched for over a century in the cultural, political, and economic fabric of multilateralism (as discussed in Chapter 1). The drug control conventions are among the most widely ratified treaties in the world. The 1961 Single Convention on Narcotic Drugs counts 154 state parties, the 1971 Convention on Psychotropic Substances has 184, and the 1988 UN Convention against Illicit Traffic in Narcotic Drugs and Psychotropic Substances, 192. Few other international agreements enjoy such near-universal engagement. For comparison, the Rome Statute of the International Criminal Court has 125 states parties.

Yet, widespread ratification does not imply widespread compliance. A glance through the annexes of the INCB's annual reports reveals that not all countries submit complete data on the consumption and distribution of scheduled substances for legitimate uses. Many provide partial reports or leave the forms entirely blank. The problem is compounded by the nature of prohibition itself. With the majority of drug activity occurring in illegal markets, data collection is severely limited. Disaggregated legal data beyond seizures and arrests are rare, making it difficult to understand the actual scope of the problem or how to respond to it effectively. Despite these longstanding issues, serious global debate about the need to reform international drug control law and mechanisms has only intensified since 2008 (with some prominent voices raising the issue much earlier, but being highly marginalized, such as Libertarian politicians or civil society activists). What follows is an examination of how this shift occurred, what reform options exist, and why none appear imminent. I think it is also important to remind that the reform options discussed globally and put forward target mainly the prohibition basis of international drug law, a debate that came about since countries started to legalize drugs (mainly cannabis) and control their production and retail for non-medical uses.

## The State of Confrontation of Reformers versus Status Quo Defenders

As an observer, researcher, and practitioner of the international drug control regime and its governance for over a decade, this section is based on lived experience and many observations made inside the system. It is a tale of reform advocacy versus status quo defense. It captures the last 15 years of an intense debate in global drug fora, fought fiercely without much scrutiny from the outside world.

The roots of this confrontation, however, extend further back. In 1998, amid rising global levels of drug production, consumption, trafficking, and violence, the international community convened a second UNGASS on the world drug problem[3] (the first, held in 1990, had been prompted by the escalation of cartel violence in Colombia and led to the creation of the United Nations Drug Control Program [UNDCP] which later became UNODC).

The 1998 UNGASS culminated in a bold political declaration to "eliminate or significantly reduce" the non-medical production, consumption, and trafficking of drugs and their precursors within a decade. This was to be achieved through a tripartite strategy based on demand reduction, supply reduction, and international judicial cooperation.[4] The framework emphasized criminalization, coercive enforcement, and transnational coordination. It was launched under the slogan "A Drug-Free World: We Can Do It,"[5] a phrase whose rhetorical optimism soon gave way to empirical complexity.

By the late 2000s, the promised outcomes had not materialized. There was no reduction but rather an increase in the availability, trafficking, or use of controlled substances. Instead, the unintended consequences of global prohibition became more pronounced, including the growth of illicit markets, increased violence in producer and transit countries, mass incarceration in consumer states, and measurable harm to public health systems. Nevertheless, in 2009 and after a year of debates since the expiration of the UNGASS 1998 political commitments, the international community reaffirmed its commitment to a drug-free world by 2019,[6] reiterating the 1998 framework almost verbatim in a new political declaration. This act of recommitment, despite mounting empirical evidence of rising issues, marked the beginning of a deepening fracture in the international consensus.

All governments endorsed the 2009 Political Declaration at the CND, but many did so while expressing concern over the commitments' growing misalignment with on-the-ground realities.[7] The rigidity of the framework, the lack of meaningful evaluation mechanisms, and the absence of space for national-level policy experimentation were cited repeatedly. These critiques intensified in parallel with the deterioration of public security in parts of Latin

America. After Mexico's Calderón administration militarized its drug strategy in 2006, violence surged, drawing regional and international attention to the limits of enforcement-based models. This fragility of consensus had already become apparent in the lead-up to the 2009 Political Declaration. During negotiations, delegates failed to reach an agreement on the inclusion of harm reduction, a concept increasingly central to public health approaches but still politically divisive. The deadlock was so pronounced that Germany, along with 24 other countries, issued a formal interpretative statement to clarify their continued commitment to harm reduction, effectively bypassing the official text.[8] Moreover, Bolivia took the unprecedented step of withdrawing from the drug control conventions altogether, only to rejoin later with a specific reservation protecting the traditional and cultural use of the coca leaf (more on this in the next section). These developments, technical in appearance, marked a growing instability in the legal and political coherence of the international drug control regime. They underscored a simple but crucial point that even among signatories, the consensus underpinning the system was no longer uniform.

In 2012, Mexico, Colombia, and Guatemala, countries bearing the brunt of this violence, formally called for a new UNGASS. Their request was supported by over ninety-five other countries, signaling a growing appetite for reform.[9] The resulting 2016 UNGASS produced a more complex outcome through a seven-pillar framework that expanded the scope of international drug policy to include access to essential medicines, human rights, responses to emerging synthetic substances, dark web markets, and sustainable alternatives to illicit crop cultivation, all negotiated through the CND.[10] These additions did not replace the original three pillars but layered new concerns atop an old foundation.

The negotiations leading to this outcome exposed structural tensions within the multilateral system. Countries began to coalesce into informal blocs. On one side were states advocating for a health-oriented, evidence-based, and rights-respecting approach, among them Canada, Colombia, Mexico, and several Western European nations. On the other side were those defending the traditional prohibitionist architecture, led by the Russian Federation, Iran, and a range of Asian and Middle Eastern governments. These divisions were not merely ideological but reflected broader geopolitical alignments and differing assessments of institutional legitimacy and national interest.

The evolving position of the United States further complicated the picture. Historically the principal sponsor of the global war on drugs, the United States began to face internal contradictions. The legalization of recreational cannabis in several U.S. states conflicted with federal law and with the international treaties the United States had long championed. At the same time, the opioid epidemic, driven not by trafficking networks alone but by regulatory failure and the "iron rule of prohibition"[11] undermined its moral authority in drug control discussions. American officials maintained that federal law remained compliant with the conventions, but this position was increasingly unconvincing to both allies and adversaries.

In this context, Ambassador William Brownfield, then Assistant Secretary of State for the Bureau of International Narcotics and Law Enforcement Affairs, articulated what became known as the "Brownfield Doctrine."[12] This four-point strategy attempted to preserve the architecture of the drug control conventions while promoting a more flexible interpretation, allowing room for divergent national approaches, including cannabis legalization. It emphasized the need to focus on combating transnational criminal networks rather than regulating domestic drug use. Despite its pragmatism, the doctrine failed to persuade the INCB, which continued to assert since then that legalization for non-medical use violated international law, and it did little to placate governments committed to strict treaty interpretation.

As U.S. influence waned, Russia emerged as a more assertive actor.[13] It leveraged the CND, where the UNGASS 2016 outcome document was negotiated and finalized, as a platform to reinforce traditional priorities. Through procedural mechanisms, such as channeling inputs through the rigid and outdated UN regional group system, Russia ensured that its position and those of its allies were overrepresented. Sharing its priorities through the Eastern European group, Russia emphasized the failure of global drug control to meet its original goals and blamed that failure on calls for reform. In its view, the emergence of NPS, growing critiques of the system, and shifting attitudes toward legalization were symptoms not of structural misalignment but of weakening political will.[14]

Russia's assertiveness extended beyond the UN. In 2014, as G8 chair, it placed drug cooperation at the top of its priority list, ahead of counterterrorism, disaster preparedness, and health security. A dedicated ministerial meeting was planned,[15] but the initiative collapsed following the annexation of Crimea and Russia's suspension from the G8. Still, the Russian government pivoted to the BRICS forum, using it to align key emerging economies around a conservative drug policy stance. At the 2015 BRICS summit in Ufa, Russia hosted expert meetings and secured joint statements affirming commitment to the 2009 Declaration and rejecting harm reduction models,[16] particularly opioid agonist therapy, despite WHO's classification of methadone as an essential medicine.

Russia also attempted to launch a global "anti-substitution therapy coalition," rallying support from Gulf Cooperation Council states and Central Asian governments. Interestingly, even countries with punitive domestic regimes, such as China and Iran, continued implementing methadone programs while publicly supporting Russia's broader diplomatic line. This inconsistency reflected the growing gap between international discourse and domestic practice across many governments.

Following the adoption of the UNGASS 2016 outcome document, Russia moved quickly to downplay its significance. It argued that the 2009 Political Declaration remained the superior and more legitimate instrument. When, in 2016, a month after the UNGASS, the World Health Assembly considered a non-binding resolution asking WHO to develop a health-sector strategy on drugs, Russia intervened to block the decision item outright. The measure turned more modest and intended only to offer technical guidance instead, but Russia's delegation pursued an obstructionist approach during informal negotiations, drawing public criticism and rare diplomatic rebuke during the WHA plenary.[17]

In December 2017, Russia convened a parliamentary forum attended by delegates from 43 countries, including Iran, Pakistan, Tajikistan, Afghanistan, and the Philippines. Participants pledged to oppose drug policy reform and reaffirm prohibitionist principles, creating a de facto coalition ahead of the 2019 high-level review of the 2009 Declaration.[18] Through these actions, Russia positioned itself as the de facto leader of a global anti-reform bloc during the 2010s, committed to defending prohibition as the cornerstone of international drug control.

The global drug policy debate culminated in a renewed round of decennial political commitments in 2019, framed by two significant, contrasting developments. On one side, a letter co-signed by reform-oriented governments, including Colombia, Switzerland, and Portugal, was addressed to the UN Secretary-General, urging the full mobilization of the UN system's mandates to recalibrate drug policy outcomes away from an exclusive emphasis on repression. This appeal reflected growing discomfort with a law enforcement-centric approach, particularly as advanced at the CND and staunchly upheld by UNODC (an institution whose programmatic and financial dependencies make it especially responsive to the policy preferences of its major government donors). In response, the Secretary-General brought the issue to the UN Chief Executives Board, resulting in the first-ever unified UN system position on international drug policy.[19] This milestone led to the formation of the UN System Coordination Task Team on drug-related matters, a cross-agency initiative led by UNODC and involving WHO, OHCHR, UNAIDS, UNESCO, ILO, and others.[20]

This push for systemic coherence, however, was met with a coordinated rebuttal. A counter-letter, signed by the Russian Federation, Singapore, Egypt, and a cohort of like-minded states, was also submitted to the

Secretary-General. It reasserted the centrality of the three drug-control conventions and advocated for the continued goal of eliminating illegal drug use and production, an objective unchanged since the foundational commitments of 1998 and 2009.[21] These countries, favoring continuity over reform, ultimately prevailed in shaping the official course. The result was the adoption of the 2019 Ministerial Declaration on the world drug problem, which reaffirmed the objectives of the 2009 Political Declaration (with only a slight change, as it called for a "world free of drug abuse" rather than "free of drug use"). This document, currently the primary operative framework for global drug policy, is set to remain in effect until its scheduled review in 2029. In the midst of it all, the United States remained a silent voice. In 2018, President Trump convened 122 governments at the UN General Assembly to endorse a "Global Call to Action on the World Drug Problem."[22] The initiative, bypassing the established multilateral negotiation channels of the CND, resulted in no specific breakthroughs and ultimately proved to be an effort without consequence.

Then, in early 2020, the COVID-19 pandemic struck. Practically overnight, drug policy was downgraded to a second-tier priority across much of the world. The subsequent Russian invasion of Ukraine in 2022 only reinforced this shift in focus, relegating international drug control to the margins of diplomatic and political agendas. Despite these disruptions, a notable change emerged in U.S. domestic and international postures. The Biden administration became the first in American history to formally adopt harm reduction as a component of federal drug policy. This shift resonated beyond national borders. At the CND in 2024, governments adopted for the first time ever a resolution explicitly referencing harm reduction.[23] Only Russia and China voted against. For decades, the term had been systematically excluded from any negotiated international drug policy text. The inclusion marked a symbolic but substantive departure from past orthodoxy, suggesting that even long-entrenched global frameworks can shift, if only incrementally.

The latest development occurred during the 2025 session of the CND, where Colombia successfully spearheaded a resolution calling for the establishment of an expert panel to review the multilateral drug control architecture to increase its efficacy and to propose recommendations for better international collaboration.[24] Though framed in cautious terms, with the secretariat role explicitly retained by UNODC, the resolution marked the first institutional effort to formally question the drug control mechanisms. Notably, the resolution faced opposition from both the United States and the Russian Federation. Yet it passed, backed not only by traditionally progressive actors but also by more conservative states such as Singapore and Japan.

While this was widely celebrated by reform advocates as a historic breakthrough, I remain skeptical. The past 15 years have shown that drug policy outcomes are determined less by rhetorical commitments than by the technical minutiae such as the procedural rules, the flow of financial contributions to UN drug bodies and national agencies (with a marked preference for law enforcement over health and social services), and the enduring influence of geopolitical alignments. Even if the expert panel is now on paper, the probability remains high that its composition, agenda, and eventual recommendations will be shaped, if not outright dominated, by the defenders of the status quo. Those actors who consistently invest the most and the longest (those who do not question the international framework even when national majority changes occur) in preserving the existing legal framework implementation are also those most capable of shaping the future of its so-called reform.

In today's shifting geopolitical landscape, the debate over international drug law reform continues to unfold across regions, institutions, and political traditions. What emerges is not a simple binary, but a layered spectrum of national interests, institutional inertia, and conflicting interpretations of shared legal obligations. At its core, the international drug control regime remains a mirror of global power dynamics, shaped by the preferences of its most invested actors, locked in a framework that resists adaptation, yet cannot fully ignore the mounting pressure for change that it attempts to absorb.

## Existing Legal Options

Currently, and against this backdrop of mounting tensions between countries at the CND and other multilateral fora, the options for reforming the three international drug control conventions remain narrow, with each path presenting its own distinct set of serious political and legal obstacles. Again, this debate has risen in significance in relation to cannabis, especially for states that have legalized or are moving toward legalizing non-medical drug use since the mid-2010s.

The first option, amending the international drug control conventions, exists in theory, but has remained largely dormant in practice. Under current rules, such amendments require only a simple majority in the UN General Assembly or during a specially convened Conference of the Parties. The legal framework is explicit. The Commentary on the 1961 Single Convention notes that "the General Assembly may itself take the initiative in amending the Convention, either by itself adopting the revisions, or by calling a Plenipotentiary Conference for this purpose."[25] In procedural terms, this route is relatively straightforward. In political terms, it is anything but. Despite decades of acknowledged shortcomings in the drug control regime, the willingness to initiate such formal reform at the multilateral level remains minimal, if nonexistent.

The path exists. What is missing is the political will to walk it. But even if that will emerged, it is far from clear that it would lead to more humane, liberal, or effective outcomes (the three not being mutually exclusive). In today's fractured geopolitical climate, where multilateralism itself is under pressure, opening the door to amendment may well result in more restrictive norms, not less. The opportunity for reform could easily become a platform for retrenchment, where more conservative positions prevail, human rights considerations are sidelined, and the apparatus of repression is further legitimized.

The second option, amendments to the current scheduling system, which classifies substances based on their perceived dangerousness through CND approval, is simple in theory, yet as impractical as the first option in real-world terms. According to the 1961 Convention, a simple majority among CND's 53 member states is required to adopt a WHO scheduling recommendation; the 1971 Convention demands a two-thirds majority. In principle, countries could opt to leave the conventions intact while simply de-scheduling certain drugs, thereby reclaiming more national autonomy over their regulation and their control, from enforcement to consumption. On the surface, this might seem like a straightforward route, particularly for substances like cannabis for non-medical use. However, such a move could create immense confusion. While some countries might benefit from de-scheduling, the broader repercussions could be far more disruptive. The lack of a clear, globally recognized framework could undermine access to controlled medicines for legitimate medical uses (as explored in Chapter 2), potentially exacerbating some of the very key problems any reform is meant to address.

A third route for reform, the withdrawal from the international drug conventions followed by re-accession with a reservation, has precedent, but it is far from straightforward. Bolivia provides the only successful example to date, having rejoined the 1961 Single Convention with a reservation allowing for the traditional chewing of coca leaves. The legal framework for such a maneuver exists. Article 49 of the Single Convention permits reservations for traditional uses, but only if those practices were permitted in the concerned territory on or before 1 January 1961. This clause presents a substantial barrier for cannabis or psychedelic legalization, for example, particularly in countries where traditional cannabis use was either not formally recognized or explicitly prohibited at that date.

In 2011, Bolivia proposed an amendment to the Convention, seeking to remove the requirement that coca leaf chewing be abolished. Article 49 allowed only a temporary exemption, mandating that such practices be eliminated within 25 years (since the entry into force of the convention in 1964, meaning by the end of 1989). Under the amendment procedure, Bolivia's request would have been automatically adopted unless a third of state parties objected. When sufficient support failed to materialize, Bolivia chose instead to denounce the Convention and apply for re-accession with a specific reservation on coca chewing. According to treaty rules, such re-accession could be blocked if one-third of state parties (62 out of 184) objected. No such opposition materialized. Bolivia rejoined the Convention in 2013, with its reservation intact.[26]

This precedent illustrates both the legal complexity and geopolitical delicacy of treaty reform. It also makes clear that while technically feasible, the pathway is politically narrow and structurally resistant to broader reinterpretations, especially for other substances, where the historical record of traditional use does not align with the Convention's temporal requirements.

The fourth option, unilateral noncompliance is, at best, a temporary and uneasy posture. Under this approach, countries openly acknowledge their deviation from the three drug conventions, while maintaining rhetorical support for the treaties broader objectives. This strategy rests on the idea that states can, in good faith, diverge from certain treaty provisions on the basis of evolving national priorities, human rights obligations, or public health imperatives, all while avoiding formal withdrawal or legal reinterpretation.[27] Yet this approach raises obvious contradictions. International law is built on consent and reciprocity. States voluntarily subscribe to treaty regimes and are expected to comply with their terms, even when doing so constrains elements of domestic sovereignty. A posture of selective adherence undermines the legitimacy not only of the drug control regime but of international law as a whole.

Nevertheless, there are two sides to this option. On one hand, while some countries may consider unilateral noncompliance a pragmatic stopgap, especially in the absence of viable reform avenues, it is not a stable foundation for long-term policy. It leaves states in legal limbo, exposes them to diplomatic friction, and contributes to the erosion of multilateral norms. Over time, it also invites fragmentation, where each government interprets obligations based on convenience rather than commitment. In this light, unilateral noncompliance may be tactically useful, but it is strategically flawed. It buys time, but it does not solve the problem. Like a leaking dam held together with tape, it may work until it doesn't. On the other hand, tensions between legal compliance and policy necessity are not new, especially under a regime increasingly misaligned with contemporary realities.

As one legal analysis aptly argues, noncompliance, particularly operational noncompliance, is not simply a sign of failure but can be a functional component of international legal systems that lack strong enforcement mechanisms.[28] Dismissing all operational noncompliance overlooks its potential role in advancing legal evolution, testing the boundaries of outdated norms, and even reinforcing the relevance of the law itself. In this view, certain forms of noncompliance may actually serve broader community policies and catalyze necessary reform, especially in fields where international legal regimes have grown stagnant such as drug policy, where the dissonance between treaty commitments and domestic realities widens. Ignoring this dynamic risks reducing the global normative framework to a symbolic relic, unable to adapt or respond to emerging trends and challenges. It is notable that this is the option currently favored by countries that are misaligned with the drug conventions' obligations by legalizing cannabis for non-medical use, including Canada, Uruguay, or to some extent Germany.

The fifth option, the application of inter se agreements, offers a legally grounded yet politically demanding pathway for reform. Allowed under Article 41 of the 1969 Vienna Convention on the Law of Treaties, this approach enables a group of like-minded countries that are parties to a convention to amend it among themselves, without altering obligations toward states not party to the modification.[29] In theory, this would allow a subset of nations to legally remove themselves from some international legal obligations regarding controls of psychoactive substances, including legalization, while preserving the international prohibitionist framework for others. The legal mechanics are clear; the political will, however, is not.

This approach is not without precedent. As the international regime ossifies, and more jurisdictions openly disregard treaty prohibitions, especially regarding cannabis, a structured, sustainable mechanism for their national laws becomes more pressing. This option has been offered by some of the most respected figures in international drug policy analysis and studies, including Dave Bewley-Taylor, Martin Jelsma, and Neil Boister, and for that same reason requires attention. According to their analysis, inter se agreements offer a middle road between rigid treaty compliance and the rising tide of unilateral, often messy, legal reinterpretations. They also sidestep the political impossibility of reaching a global consensus to amend the existing conventions, a scenario that remains improbable in the foreseeable geopolitical context. Importantly, such a mechanism would demand a high level of coordination and mutual commitment. The authors remind that it requires participating governments to reaffirm core treaty principles, such as the aim to promote health and welfare, while charting a new legal space for reform. In doing so, states would create what is in effect a "multi-speed" drug control system within the bounds of international law, rather than through its circumvention.[30]

If inter se modification is the most legally coherent of the available reform mechanisms, it does not imply ease. It calls for political courage, legal clarity, and a commitment to cooperative, rules-based multilateralism, qualities increasingly rare in today's fragmented international system. Moreover, the authors remind that inter se modification of the conventions could also create a regulated international trade in non-medical drugs. This could open new economic spaces for traditional producers in low- and middle-income countries, giving them access to the emerging licit markets in Europe and North America, an outcome the current system categorically prevents. Yet one must ask, soberly and without romanticism, whether the creation of a global non-medical cannabis market—for example, a subject that now occupies so much political and commercial energy and capital—can truly be considered a reform of international drug control. Its scope is narrow, its beneficiaries numerous but still selective. It does not address the structural shortcomings of the regime, including the public health crises exacerbated by repressive policies, the persistent violations of human rights, nor the insistent inaccessibility to essential controlled medicines in many parts of the world. Worse still, it risks obscuring the broader picture. By removing cannabis consumers, who account for over 70 percent of all reported drug use globally, from the realm of criminalization, this development may appear as progress. And indeed, for those individuals involved in it, it is. But in doing so, it risks leaving intact the very machinery of repression, now concentrated on more vulnerable consumers of substances associated with far greater risks of morbidity and mortality and higher criminal punishment. In this sense, what is heralded as reform carries the risk of offering relief for some while reinforcing marginalization for many.

In sum, none of the five reform options available to countries navigating the outdated architecture of the international drug control regime offer a simple or risk-free path. Amending the conventions requires political alignment that is, under current geopolitical tensions, almost utopian. Rescheduling substances within the existing framework appears administratively easier but brings unintended consequences that could undermine access to essential medicines. The Bolivia model of denunciation and re-accession with reservations is legally viable but politically fraught and narrowly applicable. Unilateral noncompliance, while expedient, remains legally ambiguous and ultimately unsustainable. Inter se agreements may represent a legal workaround, but require significant coordination, political will, and a shared long-term vision, none of which are guaranteed. Each path reveals the structural rigidity of a system established in a different century, under different assumptions. Reform, it turns out, is both necessary and deeply constrained. And whether any of these options leads to better outcomes is not a question of legal architecture alone, but of political courage, economic interest, and above all, clarity of purpose.

# CONCLUSION

## The Time Is Not Ripe

For all the political declarations, expert panels, and multilateral resolutions, the international drug control regime has proven remarkably resilient, less because of broad-based support than because of structural design. The momentum behind reform, though real, has repeatedly fallen short of structural transformation. The architecture of the system, the three conventions, the institutions, the procedures, remains largely intact. Despite the accumulation of critique, the time for true reform has not yet come. The time, as it stands, is simply not ripe.

This is not for lack of effort. Over the past two decades, networks of people who use drugs, civil society, international institutions, and several governments have produced a steady stream of critiques, policy innovations, and alternative models, from health-based responses to calls for legal regulation. But the contradictions between these initiatives and the foundational logic of the system have only grown more visible. As shown in this book, the consensus around prohibition has long started wobbling. Yet the formal structure of drug control continues to treat this consensus as real and operative. It is a system premised on the eradication of non-medical drug use, while the world it seeks to govern grows increasingly diverse in its policy approaches and domestic choices.

The reasons for this persistence are not mysterious. The regime is built to resist change. Institutions like the CND operate largely through consensus, allowing the most conservative actors to block reform. The INCB continues to interpret the conventions to the letter, limiting the space for experimentation. UNODC, dependent on earmarked funding and donor preferences, cannot afford to stray too far from the status quo. And WHO simply has too much on its hands to fully commit to drug policy. Even modest steps, like removing cannabis from Schedule IV of the 1961 Single Convention[1] or introducing harm reduction language, require years of diplomacy and pressure and remain the exception rather than the rule.

The reform landscape, in this context, is fragmented. Significant progress has been made in some areas. The adoption of harm reduction language in a CND resolution in 2024 marked a symbolic turning point, especially considering its long exclusion. Colombia's 2025 resolution calling for an expert panel to review the efficacy of the multilateral control system represents a potential step forward, though its cautious language and the oversight given to UNODC signal institutional limits. Similarly, the creation of the UN system coordination Task Team reflects a new form of cross-agency engagement, but its real influence remains modest.

Still, these developments have not generated structural change. In practice, they often function as safety valves, accommodating pressure without altering the machinery. Reform is acknowledged but compartmentalized, discussed but rarely implemented in ways that challenge the core premises of the regime. The time and energy invested in symbolic diplomacy are often greater than those invested in systemic design or implementation.

Geopolitics only reinforces this stagnation. The breakdown of global consensus on a range of international issues such as security, trade, or climate has spilled into the drug policy space. The war in Ukraine and shifting power dynamics have hardened ideological divides. The United States, while shifting domestically in 2021 and 2025, remains ambivalent internationally. Russia continues to invest diplomatically in preserving the existing architecture. China's growing influence reinforces conservatism on the global stage. Meanwhile, progressive reformers remain underfunded and outnumbered, their initiatives often blocked in technical committees or informal sessions long before reaching the formal floors of debate.

In this environment, the time for reform cannot be expected to ripen on its own. There is no natural evolution from inertia to transformation. The international drug control regime is not a failing system waiting to be replaced; it is a durable system succeeding in preserving its original purpose. It absorbs critique, adapts to surface pressures, and reasserts its core through technical processes and institutional routine. That is its genius and its failure.

States face legally viable but politically fraught paths to reform international drug law. Amending the treaties outright is procedurally possible, but politically implausible in today's fractured multilateral environment, where reform risks retrenchment rather than progress. Rescheduling substances offers a more technical route, but is often slow, contentious, and risks collateral effects such as undermining access to essential medicines. Withdrawal and re-accession with reservations is of limited applicability elsewhere due to the narrow historical criteria enshrined in the conventions. Unilateral noncompliance, where states openly deviate from certain treaty obligations while professing allegiance to broader goals, has become a common workaround, especially for countries legalizing cannabis. But this posture, while expedient, is unstable in the long term and may erode the legitimacy of the international legal order itself. Finally, the use of inter se agreements, treaty modifications among like-minded states, offers a legally coherent mechanism for coalition-based reform, yet demands high levels of coordination, trust, and political will. Each option illustrates the rigidity of a system built in another era, and while none are impossible, all confront the same dilemma, that reform is both necessary and profoundly difficult. In short, the paths are known. What is absent is not legal possibility, but geopolitical ripeness.

The lesson of the past decade is sobering. Meaningful change in global drug control will not come from rhetorical victories or isolated reforms. It will require a recalibration of the machinery itself, its funding structures, decision-making procedures, and interpretative authorities. This is not impossible, but it demands strategic, sustained effort from actors willing to invest in more than declarations. It demands coalition-building not just around ideas, but around the rules of procedure and institutional leverage points such as financing that determine what becomes policy and what becomes paperwork. For now, the international drug control regime remains a reflection of its most invested participants. It resists change, not because it is broken, but because it is working precisely as designed. In this context, delay is not incidental. It is policy.

# REFERENCES


## Introduction

1. UNODC. (2024). *World Drug Report 2024.* Vienna: UN Office on Drugs and Crime. Available from: https://www.unodc.org/documents/data-and-analysis/WDR_2024/WDR24_Key_findings_and_conclusions.pdf.

## Chapter 1

1. *The International Drug Control Conventions.* New York: United Nations. Available from: https://www.unodc.org/documents/commissions/CND/Int_Drug_Control_Conventions/Ebook/The_International_Drug_Control_Conventions_E.pdf.
2. UNODC. (2008). *A Century of International Drug Control.* Vienna: UN Office on Drugs and Crime. Available from: https://www.unodc.org/documents/data-and-analysis/Studies/100_Years_of_Drug_Control.pdf.
3. UNODC. (2019). *International Drug Control Conventions, Schedules/Tables and Control Regimes.* Vienna: UN Office on Drugs and Crime. Available from: https://www.unodc.org/documents/commissions/CND/Scheduling_Resource_Material/Scheduling_Control_Regimes.pdf.
4. Bewley-Taylor, D.R., Jelsma, M. (2012). "Regime Change: Re-visiting the 1961 Single Convention on Narcotic Drugs." *International Journal of Drug Policy*, 23(1): 72–81. https://doi.org/10.1016/j.drugpo.2011.08.003.
5. *Single Convention on Narcotic Drugs of 1961*, Article 49. New York: United Nations. Available from: https://www.unodc.org/pdf/convention_1961_en.pdf.
6. Renborg, B.A. (1964). "The Grand Old Men of the League of Nations, What They Achieved. Who They Were." *Bulletin on Narcotics.* Vienna: UN Office on Drugs and Crime. Available from: https://www.unodc.org/unodc/en/data-and-analysis/bulletin/bulletin_1964-01-01_4_page002.html.
7. Sánchez Avilés, C., Ditrych, O. (2020). "The Evolution of International Drug Control under the United Nations." In Bewley-Taylor, D.R., Tinasti, K. (Eds.). *Research Handbook on International Drug Policy.* Cheltenham: Edward Elgar Publishing: 19-37.
8. *Convention on Psychotropic Substances of 1971.* New York: United Nations. Available from: https://www.unodc.org/pdf/convention_1971_en.pdf.
9. Boister, N. (2001). *Penal Aspects of the UN Drug Conventions.* The Hague and Boston: Kluwer Law International.

10. *United Nations Convention against Illicit Traffic in Narcotic Drugs and Psychotropic Substances, 1988*. Vienna: United Nations. Available from: https://www.incb.org/documents/PRECURSORS/1988_CONVENTION/1988Convention_E.pdf.
11. The first World Drug Report was published by the UNDCP in 1997, and has been a flagship UNODC annual publication since 2004. *Previous World Drug Reports and Global Illicit Drug Trends (its predecessor)*. Available from: https://wdr.unodc.org/wdr2020/en/previous-reports.html.
12. UNODC. (2006). *Multilingual Dictionary of Narcotic Drugs and Psychotropic Substances under International Control.* Vienna: UN Office on Drugs and Crime. Available from: https://www.unodc.org/documents/scientific/MLD-06-58676_Vol_1&2_ebook.pdf.
13. INCB. (2023). *Precursors and Chemicals Frequently Used in the Illicit Manufacture of Narcotic Drugs and Psychotropic Substances.* Vienna: International Narcotics Control Board. Available from: https://unis.unvienna.org/unis/uploads/documents/2024-INCB/E_INCB2023_Precursors.pdf.
14. Jelsma, M. (2019). *Classification of Psychoactive Substances: When Science Was Left Behind.* Geneva: Global Commission on Drug Policy.
15. UN ECOSOC. (1991). *Terms of Reference of the Commission on Narcotic Drugs, Resolution 1991/38.* New York: UN Economic and Social Council. Available from: https://digitallibrary.un.org/record/127760?ln=en&v=pdf#files.
16. Crocket, A. (2010). "The Function and Relevance of the Commission in Narcotic Drugs in the Pursuit of Humane Drug Policy (or the Ramblings of a Bewildered Diplomat)." *International Journal on Human Rights and Drug Policy*, 1 (2010): 83–90.
17. Fazey, C.S.J. (2003). "The Commission on Narcotic Drugs and the United Nations International Drug Control Programme: Politics, Policies and Prospect for Change." *International Journal of Drug Policy*, 14(2): 155–169. https://doi.org/10.1016/S0955-3959(03)00004-5.
18. Bewley-Taylor, D.R. (2012). *International Drug Control: Consensus Fractured.* Cambridge: Cambridge University Press.
19. INCB. *Mandate and Functions.* Vienna: International Narcotics Control Board. Available from: https://www.incb.org/incb/en/about/mandate-functions.html.
20. Bewley-Taylor, *International Drug Control: Consensus Fractured.*
21. WHO. (2010). *Guidance on the WHO Review of Psychoactive Substances for International Control.* Geneva: World Health Organization. Available from: https://www.who.int/publications/i/item/9789241500555.
22. Expert Committee on Drug Dependence. (2019). *WHO Review of Cannabis and Cannabis-related Substances.* Geneva: World Health Organization. Available from: https://www.who.int/teams/health-product-and-policy-standards/controlled-substances/who-review-of-cannabis-and-cannabis-related-substances.
23. Walsh, J., Jelsma, M. *Coca Chronicles: Monitoring the UN Coca Review.* Amsterdam: Transnational Institute. Available from: https://www.tni.org/en/article/coca-chronicles-monitoring-the-un-coca-review.
24. McAllister, W.B. (2020). "Foundations of the International Drug Control Regime: Nineteenth Century to the Second World War." In Bewley-Taylor, D.R., Tinasti, K. (Eds.). *Research Handbook on International Drug Policy.* Cheltenham: Edward Elgar Publishing: 2-28.
25. Castairs, C. (2005). "The Stages of the International Drug Control System." *Drug and Alcohol Review*, 24: 57–65. https://doi.org/10.1080/09595230500125179.

26. McAllister, "Foundations of the International Drug Control Regime: Nineteenth Century to the Second World War": 4.
27. The countries represented were Austria-Hungary, China, France, Great Britain, Germany, Italy, Japan, Holland, Persia, Portugal, Russia, and Siam. The International Opium Commission was proposed by the United States. *Report to the Secretary of State on the Second International Opium Conference by the American Delegates: Hamilton Wright, Lloyd Bryce, Gerrit John Kollen.* (1913). Office of the Historian, U.S. Department of State. Available from: https://history.state.gov/historicaldocuments/frus1913/d229.
28. Huang, Y. (2023). "Resilient Drug Economy and Politicised Control: The Rise and Fall of the Administrative Bureau of Prohibited Drugs in China, 1922–1925." *Journal of Illicit Economies and Development*, 5(2): 54–68. https://doi.org/10.31389/jied.198.
29. *International Opium Convention, 1912.* Geneva: League of Nations. Available from: https://treaties.un.org/doc/Treaties/1922/01/19220123%2006-31%20AM/Ch_VI_2p.pdf.
30. Collins, J. (2021). *Legalising the Drug Wars: A Regulatory History of UN Drug Control.* Cambridge: Cambridge University Press.
31. Wright, Q. (1934). "The Narcotics Convention of 1931." *The American Journal of International Law*, 28(3): 475–486. https://doi.org/10.2307/2190375.
32. *International Opium Convention, 1925.* Geneva: League of Nations. Available from: https://treaties.un.org/doc/Treaties/1925/02/19250219%2006-36%20AM/Ch_VI_6_6a_6bp.pdf.
33. McAllister, "Foundations of the International Drug Control Regime: Nineteenth Century to the Second World War": 11.
34. Boister, N. (1997). "The Historical Development of International Legal Measures to Suppress Illicit Drug Trafficking." *The Comparative and International Law Journal of Southern Africa*, 30(1): 1–21.
35. *Convention for Limiting the Manufacture and Regulating the Distribution of Narcotic Drugs, 1931.* Geneva: League of Nations. Available from: https://treaties.un.org/doc/Treaties/1931/07/19310713%2006-44%20AM/Ch_VI_8_ap.pdf.
36. McAllister, "Foundations of the International Drug Control Regime: Nineteenth Century to the Second World War": 15.
37. Wakabayashi, B.T. (2012). "From Peril to Profit: Opium in Late-Edo to Meiji Eyes." In Brook, T., Carr, P., Kefalas, M. (Eds.). *Opium Regimes: China, Britain, and Japan, 1839–1952.* Oakland: online edition, California Scholarship Online. https://doi.org/10.1525/california/9780520220096.003.0021.
38. McAllister, "Foundations of the International Drug Control Regime: Nineteenth Century to the Second World War": 16.
39. Starke, J.G. (1937). "The Convention of 1936 for the Suppression of the Illicit Traffic in Dangerous Drugs." *The American Journal of International Law*, 31(1): 31–43. https://doi.org/10.2307/2190712.
40. *Convention of 1936 for the Suppression of the Illicit Traffic in Dangerous Drugs.* Geneva: League of Nations. Available from: https://treaties.un.org/doc/Treaties/1936/06/19360626%2006-49%20AM/Ch_VI_12_ap.pdf.

## Chapter 2

1. UNODC. (2008). *The World Drug Report 2008.* Vienna: UN Office on Drugs and Crime. Available from: https://www.unodc.org/documents/wdr/WDR_2008/WDR_2008_eng_web.pdf.
2. Mavrellis, C. (2017). *Transnational Crime and the Developing World.* Washington, DC: Global Financial Integrity. Available from: https://gfintegrity.org/wp-content/uploads/2017/03/Transnational_Crime-final.pdf.
3. Reitano, T., Hunter, M. (2018). *The Crime-Development Paradox: Organized Crime and the SDGs.* ENACT. Available from: https://globalinitiative.net/wp-content/uploads/2018/02/ENACT-Continental-Report-02-14Feb1145.pdf.
4. *Las 50 ciudades más violentas del mundo 2024.* (2025). Mexico City: Seguridad, Justicia y Paz. Available from: https://geoenlace.net/seguridadjusticiaypaz/webpage/timeline.php.
5. *The Alternative World Drug Report.* (2012). London: Count the Costs. Available from: https://www.unodc.org/documents/ungass2016/Contributions/Civil/Count-the-Costs-Initiative/AWDR-exec-summary.pdf
6. EUROPOL. (2021). *Enterprising Criminals—Europe's Fight against the Global Networks of Financial and Economic Crime.* Brussels: European Union Agency for Law Enforcement Cooperation. Available from: https://www.europol.europa.eu/cms/sites/default/files/documents/efecc_-_enterprising_criminals_-_europes_fight_against_the_global_networks_of_financial_and_economic_crime_.pdf.
7. Reitano, T. (2022). *The Challenges of Responding to IFFs Where Political Will Is Absent: A Synthesis Evidence Review.* Birmingham: SOC ACE. Available from: https://www.birmingham.ac.uk/documents/college-social-sciences/government-society/publications/political-will-absent-briefing.pdf.
8. WACD. (2014). *Not Just In Transit: Drugs, the State and Society in West Africa.* Geneva: Kofi Annan Foundation. Available from: https://www.kofiannanfoundation.org/wp-content/uploads/2024/04/West-Africa-Commission-on-Drugs-report.pdf.
9. Tinasti, K. (2020). "The Neo-Patrimonial 'Use' of Drug Policy in Electoral Processes." *International Development Policy*, 12. https://doi.org/10.4000/poldev.3842.
10. Green, M.A. (2024). *Mexico's Historic Elections—and Political Violence.* Washington, DC: Wilson Center. Available from: https://www.wilsoncenter.org/blog-post/mexicos-historic-elections-and-political-violence.
11. PRI. (2024). *Global Prison Trends 2024.* London: Penal Reform International. Available from: https://cdn.penalreform.org/wp-content/uploads/2024/09/PRI_Global-prison-trends-report-2024_EN.pdf.
12. HRI. (2025). *The Death Penalty for Drug Offences: Global Overview 2024.* London: Harm Reduction International. Available from: https://hri.global/wp-content/uploads/2025/03/HRI-GlobalOverview-2024-FINAL.pdf.
13. INCB. (2016). *INCB Reiterates Its Call to States to Consider the Abolition of the Death Penalty for Drug-Related Offences.* Vienna: International Narcotics Control Board.
14. OHCHR. (2015). *Using the Death Penalty to Fight Drug Crimes Violates International Law, UN Rights Experts Warn World Day Against the Death Penalty.* Geneva: Office of the High Commissioner for Human Rights.
15. ICC. (2025). *The Prosecutor vs. Rodrigo Roa Duterte, ICC-01/21-01/25.* The Hague: International Criminal Court. Available from: https://www.icc-cpi.int/philippines/duterte.

16. Eligh J. (2019). *A Militarized Political Weapon: The Philippines' War on Drugs*. Geneva: The Global Initiative Against Transnational Organized Crime. Available from: https://globalinitiative.net/the-philippines-war-on-drugs/.
17. HRC. (2015). *Contribution of the Human Rights Council to the Special Session of the General Assembly on the World Drug Problem of 2016, Resolution A/HRC/28/L.22*. Geneva: Human Rights Council.
18. *Report of the Special Rapporteur on Torture and Other Cruel, Inhuman or Degrading Treatment or Punishment, Juan E. Méndez, Report A/HRC/22/53*. (2013). Geneva: Human Rights Council.
19. *Report of the Special Rapporteur on the Right of Everyone to the Enjoyment of the Highest Attainable Standard of Physical and Mental Health, Note by the Secretary-General A/65/255*. (2010). New York: United Nations General Assembly.
20. *Report of the Special Rapporteur on Violence against Women, Its Causes and Consequences, Rashida Manjoo, Note by the Secretary-General A/68/340*. (2013). New York: United Nations General Assembly.
21. *Study on Arbitrary Detention Relating to Drug Policies, A/HRC/47/40*. (2021). Geneva: Human Rights Council.
22. *Drug Laws must be Amended to "Combat Racial Discrimination," UN Experts Say*. (2019). Geneva: Office of the High Commissioner for Human Rights.
23. *UN Experts Urge the Philippines to Stop Unlawful Killings of People Suspected of Drug-Related Offences*. (2016). Geneva: Office of the High Commissioner for Human Rights.
24. OHCHR. (2023). *Human Rights Challenges in Addressing and Countering all Aspects of the World Drug Problem, A/HRC/54/53*. Geneva: Office of the High Commissioner for Human Rights. Available from: https://docs.un.org/en/A/HRC/54/53.
25. *Single Convention on Narcotic Drugs of 1961*, Preamble. New York: United Nations. Available from: https://www.unodc.org/pdf/convention_1961_en.pdf.
26. WHO. (1946). *Constitution of the World Health Organization*. Geneva: World Health Organization. Available from: http://www.who.int/governance/eb/who_constitution_en.pdf.
27. WHO's Director-General and UNODC's Executive Director signed in June 2018, in Geneva, a WHO-UNODC Memorandum of Understanding to facilitate the collaboration between the two organizations on the health dimensions of the international drug control regime. Available from: https://www.who.int/publications/m/item/mou-who-unodc-controlled-substances.
28. UNAIDS. (2009). *WHO, UNODC, UNAIDS Technical Guide for Countries to Set Targets for Universal Access to HIV Prevention, Treatment and Care for Injecting Drug Users*. Geneva: World Health Organization, United Nations Office on Drugs and Crime, Joint United Nations Program on HIV/AIDS. Revised in 2012. Available from: https://www.unodc.org/documents/hiv-aids/idu_target_setting_guide.pdf.
29. WHO. (2022). *Global Health Sector Strategies on, Respectively, HIV, Viral Hepatitis and Sexually Transmitted Infections for the Period 2022–2030*. Geneva: World Health Organization. Available from: https://iris.who.int/bitstream/handle/10665/360348/9789240053779-eng.pdf?sequence=1.
30. UNAIDS. (2024). *Global AIDS Targets 2025 for People Who Use Drugs: Where Are We Now?* Geneva: Joint United Nations Program on HIV/AIDS. Available from: https://www.unaids.org/sites/default/files/media_asset/global-AIDS-targets-2025-for-people-who-use-drugs-where-are-we-now_en.pdf

31. UNAIDS. (2024). *2024 Global AIDS Report—The Urgency of Now: AIDS at a Crossroads.* Geneva: Joint United Nations Program on HIV/AIDS. Available from: https://www.unaids.org/sites/default/files/media_asset/2024-unaids-global-aids-update-eeca_en.pdf.
32. UNODC. (2024). *World Drug Report 2024.* Vienna: UN Office on Drugs and Crime. Available from: https://www.unodc.org/documents/data-and-analysis/WDR_2024/WDR24_Key_findings_and_conclusions.pdf.
33. *Political Declaration on HIV and AIDS: Ending Inequalities and Getting on Track to End AIDS by 2030, Resolution A/RES/284.* (2021). New York: United Nations General Assembly.
34. UNAIDS. (2014). *Agenda Item 11: Halving HIV Transmission among People Who Inject Drugs, Background Note.* Geneva: Joint United Nations Programme on HIV/AIDS.
35. Dutta, A., Wirtz, A., Stanciole, A., Oelrichs, R., et al. (2013). *The Global Epidemics among People Who Inject Drugs.* Washington, DC: The World Bank.
36. WHO. (2009). *Guidelines for the Psychosocially Assisted Pharmacological Treatment of Opioid Dependence.* Geneva: World Health Organization.
37. Shoptaw, S., Montgomery, B., Williams, C.T., El-Bassel, N. et al. (2013). "Not Just the Needle: The State of HIV Prevention Science among Substance Users and Future Directions." *Journal of Acquired Immune Deficiency Syndromes*, 63(2): S174–S178. https://doi.org/10.1097/QAI.0b013e3182987028.
38. *Statistiques et analyses concernant VIH/IST.* Bern: Swiss Federal Office of Public Health. Available from: https://www.bag.admin.ch/dam/bag/fr/dokumente/mt/p-und-p/hiv-sti-statistiken-analysen-und-trends/sexuell-uebertragene-infektionen-hepbc-2023.pdf.download.pdf/infections-sexuellement-transmissibles-hepbc-2023.pdf.
39. Schwartländer, B., Stover, J., Hallett, T., Atun, R. et al. (2011). "Towards an Improved Investment Approach for an Effective Response to HIV/AIDS." *Lancet.* http://dx.doi.org/10.1016/S0140-6736(11)60702-2.
40. HRI. (2024). *The Cost of Complacency: A Harm Reduction Funding Crisis.* London: Harm Reduction International. Available from: https://hri.global/wp-content/uploads/2024/06/HRI_Funding-Report-2024_AW_080724.pdf.
41. HRI. (2024). *The Global State of Harm Reduction 2024.* London: Harm Reduction International. Available from: https://hri.global/wp-content/uploads/2024/10/GSR24_full-document_12.12.24_B.pdf.
42. Colledge-Frisby, S., Ottaviano, S., Webb, P., Grebely, J. et al. (2023). "Global Coverage of Interventions to Prevent and Manage Drug-Related Harms among People Who Inject Drugs: A Systematic Review." *Lancet Global Health*, 11(5): e673–e683. https://doi.org/10.1016/S2214-109X(23)00058-X.
43. UNODC, *World Drug Report 2024.*
44. EMCDDA. (2015). *Perspectives on Drugs: Hepatitis C Treatment for Injecting Drug Users.* Lisbon: European Monitoring Centre for Drugs and Drug Addiction. Available from: https://www.euda.europa.eu/publications/pods/hepatitis-c-treatment_en.
45. WHO. (2012). *Guidelines for the Screening, Care and Treatment of Persons with Hepatitis C Infection.* Geneva: World Health Organization.
46. WHO. (2014). *Hepatitis, Resolution WHA67/6.* Geneva: World Health Assembly.
47. UNODC. (2017). *Promoting Measures to Prevent and Treat Viral Hepatitis C Attributable to Drug Use, Resolution 62/7.* Vienna: Commission on Narcotic Drugs.
48. WHO. (2015). *WHO's Role, Mandate and Activities to Counter the World Drug Problem: A Public Health Perspective.* Geneva: World Health Organization. Available from:

https://www.who.int/publications/m/item/who-s-role-mandate-and-activities-to-counter-the-world-drug-problem.

49. Degenhardt, L., Charlson, F., Ferrari, A.J., Satomaro, D. et al. (2018). "The Global Burden of Disease Attributable to Alcohol and Drug Use in 195 Countries and Territories, 1990–2016: A Systematic Analysis for the Global Burden of Disease Study 2016." *Lancet Psychiatry*, 5(12): 987–1012. https://doi.org/10.1016/S2215-0366(18)30337-7.
50. National Center for Health Statistics. (2024). *Provisional Drug Overdose Death Counts.* Atlanta: Centers for Disease Control.
51. DEA. (2024). *Year in Review: DEA Innovates to Fight Fentanyl.* Washington, DC: Drug Enforcement Administration.
52. *Fentanyl and Fentanyl Analogues Trafficking.* (2024). Washington, DC: United States Sentencing Commission.
53. WHO. (2016). *WHO-UNODC "Stop Overdose Safely (S-O-S)" Initiative.* Geneva: World Health Organization. Available from: https://www.who.int/initiatives/joint-unodc-who-programme-on-drug-dependence-treatment-and-care/S-O-S-initiative.
54. ONDCP. (2024). *Biden-Harris Administration Actions to Address the Overdose Epidemic.* Washington, DC: Office of National Drug Control Policy.
55. National Center for Health Statistics, *Provisional Drug Overdose Death Counts.*
56. Friedman, J., Shover, C.L. (2023). "Charting the Fourth Wave: Geographic, Temporal, Race/Ethnicity and Demographic Trends in Polysubstance Fentanyl Overdose Deaths in the United States, 2010–2021." *Addiction*, 188(12): 2477–2485. https://doi.org/10.1111/add.16318.
57. Parker, A. (2024). *US Drug Overdose Deaths Are Dropping, and Here's Why.* Washington, DC: InSight Crime.
58. UNHCR. (2021). *People Who Inject Drugs: HIV in Humanitarian Emergencies.* Geneva: The United Nations Refugee Agency. Available from: http://his.unhcr.org/aae/?page_id=426#_ftn1, accessed 2 December 2021.
59. Streel, E., Schilperoord, M. (2010). "Perspectives on Alcohol and Substance Abuse in Refugee Settings: Lessons from the Field." *Intervention*, 8(3): 268–275. https://doi.org/10.1097/WTF.0b013e328341315f.
60. Hussain, H., Qayum, A. (2006). *Situational Analysis of Drug Users in Afghan Refugees Camps of NWFP, Pakistan.* Vienna: UN Office on Drugs and Crime.
61. UNHCR. (2010). *Addressing HIV amongst Most-at-Risk Populations in Humanitarian Settings: Afghan Refugee Drug Users in Peshawar, Pakistan.* Geneva: United Nations High Commissioner for Refugees.
62. Nashed, M. (2014). *Palestinian Refugees Struggle with Drugs.* Doha: Aljazeera. Available from: http://www.aljazeera.com/news/middleeast/2014/03/palestinian-refugees-201434116578524 53.html.
63. INCB. (2025). *Narcotic Drugs/Psychotropic Substances.* Vienna: International Narcotics Control Board.
64. INCB. (2015). *Availability of Internationally Controlled Drugs: Ensuring Adequate Access for Medical and Scientific Purposes. Indispensable, Adequately Available and Not Unduly Restricted.* Vienna: International Narcotics Board, 2015.
65. Seya, M.J., Gelders, S.F.A.M., Achara, O.U., Milani, B. et al. (2011). "A First Comparison between the Consumption of and the Need for Opioid Analgesics at Country, Regional and Global Level." *Journal of Pain & Palliative Care Pharmacotherapy*, 25: 6–18. https://doi.org/10.3109/15360288.2010.536307.

66. Knaul, F.M., Farmer, P.E., Krakauer, E.L., De Lima, L. et al. (2018). "Alleviating the Access Abyss in Palliative Care and Pain Relief-an Imperative of Universal Health Coverage: The Lancet Commission Report." *Lancet*, 391(10128): 1391–1454. https://doi.org/10.1016/S0140-6736(17)32513-8.
67. *Cancer Prevention and Control, Resolution WHA58/22 (2005) / Strengthening of Palliative Care as a Component of Comprehensive Care Throughout the Life Course, Resolution WHA67/19 (2014) / Strengthening Emergency and Essential Surgical Care and Anaesthesia as a Component of Universal Health Coverage, Resolution WHA68/31.* (2015). Geneva: World Health Assembly.
68. UNGA. (2016). *Outcome Document of the Thirtieth Special Session of the General Assembly, entitled "Our Joint Commitment to Effectively Addressing and Countering the World Drug Problem."* New York: United Nations General Assembly.
69. WHO. (2017). *China Policies to Promote Local Production of Pharmaceutical Products and Protect Public Health.* Geneva: World Health Organization. Available from: https://iris.who.int/bitstream/handle/10665/336684/9789241512176-eng.pdf?sequence=1
70. UNODC. (2023). *World Drug Report 2023, the Synthetic Drug Phenomenon.* Vienna: UN Office on Drugs and Crime. Available from: https://www.unodc.org/res/WDR-2023/WDR23_B3_CH1_Synthetic_drugs.pdf.
71. UNODC, *World Drug Report 2023, the Synthetic Drug Phenomenon.*
72. Eligh, J. (2024). *Global Synthetic Drug Markets, the Present and Future.* Vienna: Global Initiative against Transnational Organized Crime. Available from: https://globalinitiative.net/wp-content/uploads/2024/03/Jason-Eligh-Global-synthetic-drug-markets-The-present-and-future-GI-TOC-March-2024.pdf.
73. Shortis, P., Aldridge, J., Barratt, M.J. (2020). "Drug Cryptomarket Futures: Structure, Function and Evolution in Response to Law Enforcement Actions." In Bewley-Taylor, D.R., Tinasti, K. (Eds.). *Research Handbook on International Drug Policy.* Cheltenham: Edward Elgar Publishing, 355–379.
74. *The Synthetic Silk Road: Tracing China's Grey-Market Precursor Chemical Trade.* (2024). Washington, DC: InSight Crime. Available from: https://insightcrime.org/investigations/synthetic-silk-road-tracing-china-grey-market-precursor-chemical-trade/.
75. Aldridge, J., Décary-Hétu, D. (2014). *Not an "Ebay for Drugs": The Cryptomarket "Silk Road" as a Paradigm Shifting Criminal Innovation.* http://dx.doi.org/10.2139/ssrn.2436643.
76. Aldridge, J., Askew, R. (2017). "Delivery Dilemmas: How Drug Cryptomarket Users Identify and Seek to Reduce their Risk of Detection by Law Enforcement." *International Journal of Drug Policy*, 41: 101–109. https://doi.org/10.1016/j.drugpo.2016.10.010.
77. Soska, K., Christin, N. (2015). "Measuring the Longitudinal Evolution of the Online Anonymous Marketplace Ecosystem." In *Proceedings of the 24th Security Symposium (USENIX Security '15), Washington, DC, 12–14 August.*
78. Branwen, G. (2019). *Darknet Market Mortality Risks.* Gwern. Net.
79. Shortis, Aldridge, Barratt, "Drug Cryptomarket Futures: Structure, Function and Evolution in Response to Law Enforcement Actions," 361.
80. Shortis, Aldridge, Barratt, "Drug Cryptomarket Futures: Structure, Function and Evolution in Response to Law Enforcement Actions," 362–363.
81. *Attorney General Sessions Announces New Tool to Fight Online Drug Trafficking.* (2018). Washington, DC: Department of Justice.

82. *J-CODE Announces 61 Arrests in its Second Coordinated Law Enforcement Operation Targeting Opioid Trafficking on the Darknet.* (2019). Washington, DC: Federal Bureau of Investigation. Available from: https://www.fbi.gov/news/press-releases/j-code-announces-61-arrests-in-its-second-coordinated-law-enforcement-operation-targeting-opioid-trafficking-on-the-darknet.
83. *Largest International Operation Against Darknet Trafficking of Fentanyl and Opioids Results in Record Arrests and Seizures.* (2023). Washington, DC: Department of Justice. Available from: https://www.justice.gov/archives/opa/pr/largest-international-operation-against-darknet-trafficking-fentanyl-and-opioids-results.
84. INCB. (2023). *Annual Report, Chapter I the Role of the Internet, Including Social Media, in Drug Trafficking and Use.* Vienna: International Narcotics Control Board. Available from: https://www.incb.org/documents/Publications/AnnualReports/Thematic_chapters/English/AR_2023_E_Chapter_I.pdf.

## Chapter 3

1. Pascual, A. (2020). *In Major Shift, UN Drug Chief Questions Whether Control Treaties Involving Cannabis Are Out of Date.* Toronto: MJ BizDaily. Available from: https://mjbizdaily.com/in-major-shift-un-drug-chief-questions-whether-control-treaties-involving-cannabis-are-out-of-date/.
2. Fedotov, Y. (2019). "The Straw Men Reigniting an 'International War on Drugs': A Case for Multilateralism." *The Brown Journal of World Affairs*, 25(2): 93–108.
3. The world drug problem is defined as "the illicit cultivation, production, manufacture, sale, demand, trafficking and distribution of narcotic drugs and psychotropic substances, including amphetamine-type stimulants, the diversion of precursors and related criminal activities"; UN. (1998). *Political Declaration, Resolution S-20/2.* New York: United Nations General Assembly.
4. UN. (1998). *Measures to Enhance International Cooperation to Counter the World Drug Problem, Resolution S-20/4.* New York: United Nations General Assembly.
5. Nougier, M. (2018). *Taking Stock: A Decade of Drug Policy—A Civil Society Shadow Report.* London: International Drug Policy Consortium.
6. UNODC. (2009). *Political Declaration and Plan of Action on International Cooperation towards an Integrated and Balanced Strategy to Counter the World Drug Problem.* Vienna: Commission on Narcotic Drugs.
7. Bewley-Taylor, D.R. (2009). "The 2009 Commission on Narcotic Drugs and its High Level Segment: More Cracks in the Vienna Consensus." *Drugs and Alcohol Today*, 9(2): 7–12. https://doi.org/10.1108/17459265200900013.
8. Bridge, M., Hallam, C., Nougier, M., et al. (2017). *Edging Forward: How the UN's Language on Drugs has Advanced Since 1990.* London: International Drug Policy Consortium.
9. UN. (2012). *International Cooperation against the World Drug Problem, Resolution A/RES/67/193.* New York: General Assembly.
10. *Our Joint Commitment to Effectively Addressing and Countering the World Drug Problem, Resolution A/S-30/L.1.* (2016). New York: General Assembly.
11. Beletsky, L., Corey, S.D. (2017). "Today's Fentanyl Crisis: Prohibition's Iron Law, Revisited." *International Journal of Drug Policy*, 46: 156–159. https://doi.org/10.1016/j.drugpo.2017.05.050.

12. Lines, R., Barrett, D. (2014). "Guest Post: Has the US just Called for Unilateral Interpretation of Multilateral Obligations?" *OpinioJuris*, December 18. Available from: http://opiniojuris.org/2014/12/18/guest-post-us-just-called-unilateral-interpretation-multilateral-obligations/.
13. Tinasti, K, Barbosa Carvalho, I. (2017). "The Influence of Global Players on the Drug Control System: An Analysis of the Role of the Russian Federation." *Drugs and Alcohol Today*, 17(2): 124–134. More information on the power balance in drug control policy ahead of UNGASS 2016 was published in The Economist (2015). *The New Drug Warriors.* May 2. Available from: https://www.economist.com/international/2015/05/02/the-new-drug-warriors.
14. UNODC. (2015). *The Russian Federation proposals for the UN General Assembly Special Session on the World Drug Problem to be held in 2016. Comprehensive Package of Contributions Input for Preparation UNGASS Outcome Document Submitted through the UNGASS Board Members.* Vienna: Commission on Narcotic Drugs.
15. *Anti-Drug Cooperation. Position Paper of Anti-Drug Agenda within the Frames of the Presidency of the G8.* (2014). Moscow: Federal Drug Control Service.
16. BRICS. (2015). *VII BRICS Summit: 2015 Ufa Declaration.* Ufa: BRICS. Available from: www.en.brics2015.ru/load/381158.
17. WHO. (2016). *Live Web Stream from Sixty-Ninth World Health Assembly (WHA69).* Available from: http://www.who.int/mediacentre/events/2016/wha69/webstreaming/en/.
18. Litavrin, M. (2017). *No to Any Humanization: How State Duma Discussed Drug Policy* (Максим Литаврин Никакой гуманизации: как в Госдуме обсудили наркополитику). Available from: https://openrussia.org/notes/716900/.
19. CEB. (2018). *United Nations System Common Position Supporting the Implementation of the International Drug Control Policy through Effective Inter-agency Collaboration, Decision CEB/2018/2.* New York: United Nations Chief Executives Board for Coordination. Available from: https://www.unsceb.org/CEBPublicFiles/CEB-2018-2-SoD.pdf.
20. UNODC. (2019). *What We Have Learned over the Last Ten Years: A Summary of Knowledge Acquired and Produced by the UN System on Drug-Related Matters.* Vienna: UN Office on Drugs and Crime. Available from: https://www.unodc.org/documents/commissions/CND/2019/Contributions/UN_Entities/What_we_have_learned_over_the_last_ten_years_-_14_March_2019_-_w_signature.pdf.
21. *Press Release on the Russia-Initiated Letter of 22 States to UN Secretary-General Antonio Guterres in Support of the UN Commission on Narcotic Drugs and the Current International System of Drug Control.* (2018). Moscow: Ministry of Foreign Affairs. Available from: https://www.mid.ru/en/foreign_policy/news/1569700/.
22. White House. (2018). *Remarks by President Trump at "Global Call to Action on the World Drug Problem" Event.* Washington, DC: White House. Available from: https://trumpwhitehouse.archives.gov/briefings-statements/remarks-president-trump-global-call-action-world-drug-problem-event/.
23. UNODC. (2024). *Preventing and Responding to Drug Overdose through Prevention, Treatment, Care, and Recovery Measures as Well as Other Public Health Interventions to Address the Harms Associated with Illicit Drug Use as Part of a Balanced, Comprehensive, Scientific Evidence-Based Approach, Resolution 67/4.* Vienna: Commission on Narcotic Drugs.
24. Fordham, A., Cots Fernandez, A. (2025). *CND68: Historic Vote Initiates Overdue Review of UN Drug Control "Machinery."* London: International Drug Policy Consortium.

Available from: https://idpc.net/blog/2025/03/cnd68-historic-vote-initiates-overdue-review-of-un-drug-control-machinery.

25. UNSG. (1973). *Commentary on the Single Convention on Narcotic Drugs, 1961* (pp. 462–463). New York: UN Secretary-General. Available from: https://www.unodc.org/documents/commissions/CND/Int_Drug_Control_Conventions/Commentaries-OfficialRecords/1961Convention/1961_COMMENTARY_en.pdf.
26. UNODC. (2013). *Bolivia to Re-accede to UN Drug Convention, While Making Exception on Coca Leaf Chewing.* Vienna: UN Office on Drugs and Crime. Available from: https://www.unodc.org/unodc/en/frontpage/2013/January/bolivia-to-re-accede-to-un-drug-convention-while-making-exception-on-coca-leaf-chewing.html.
27. Bewley-Taylor, D.R., Jelsma, M., Rolles, S., Walsh, J. (2016). *Cannabis Regulation and the UN Drug Treaties, Strategies for Reform.* Washington, DC: Washington Office on Latin America. Available from: https://www.wola.org/wp-content/uploads/2016/08/Cannabis-Regulation-and-the-UN-Drug-Treaties_June-2016_web.pdf.
28. Cogan, J.K. (2006). "Noncompliance and the International Rule of Law." *Yale Journal of International Law*, 31(1): 189–210.
29. *Vienna Convention on the Law of Treaties of 1969*, Article 41. Vienna: United Nations. Available from: https://treaties.un.org/doc/Treaties/1980/01/19800127%2000-52%20AM/Ch_XXIII_01.pdf.
30. Jelsma, M., Boister, N., Bewley-Taylor, D.R., Fitzmaurice, M., Walsh, J. (2018). *Balancing Treaty Stability and Change: Inter se Modification of the UN Drug Control Conventions to Facilitate Cannabis Regulation.* Global Drug Policy Observatory, Transnational Institute, Washington Office on Latin America. Available from: https://www.wola.org/wp-content/uploads/2018/04/FINAL_Updated.pdf.

## Conclusion

1. UNODC. (2020). *CND Votes on Recommendations for Cannabis and Cannabis-Related Substances.* Vienna: Commission on Narcotic Drugs. Available from: https://www.unodc.org/unodc/en/frontpage/2020/December/cnd-votes-on-recommendations-for-cannabis-and-cannabis-related-substances.html.

# INDEX

www.ingramcontent.com/pod-product-compliance
Lightning Source LLC
Chambersburg PA
CBHW031549270326
41937CB00046BA/551